POSITIVE DISCIPLINE
IN THE CLASSROOM

Also in the Positive Discipline Series

Positive Discipline
Jane Nelsen

Positive Discipline: The First Three Years
Jane Nelsen, Cheryl Erwin, and Roslyn Duffy

Positive Discipline for Preschoolers
Jane Nelsen, Cheryl Erwin, and Roslyn Duffy

Positive Discipline for Children with Special Needs
Jane Nelsen, Steven Foster, and Arlene Raphael

Positive Discipline: A Teacher's A–Z Guide,
Revised and Expanded 2nd Edition
Jane Nelsen, Roslyn Duffy, Linda Escobar, Kate Ortolano,
and Debbie Owen-Sohocki

Positive Discipline for A–Z, Revised and Expanded 3rd Edition
Jane Nelsen, Ed.D., Lynn Lott, M.A., M.F.T., and
H. Stephen Glenn

Positive Discipline for Single Parents
Jane Nelsen, Cheryl Erwin, and Carol Delzer

Positive Discipline for Parenting in Recovery
Jane Nelsen, Riki Intner, and Lynn Lott

Positive Discipline for Childcare Providers
Jane Nelsen and Cheryl Erwin

Positive Time-Out: And Over 50 Ways to Avoid Power Struggles
in the Home and the Classroom
Jane Nelsen

Positive Discipline for Teenagers, Revised 3rd Edition
Jane Nelsen and Lynn Lott

POSITIVE DISCIPLINE

IN THE CLASSROOM

Developing Mutual Respect, Cooperation,
and Responsibility in Your Classroom

Revised 4th Edition

JANE NELSEN, ED.D., M.F.T., LYNN LOTT, M.A., M.F.T.,

AND H. STEPHEN GLENN

THREE RIVERS PRESS · NEW YORK

Published in the United States by Three Rivers Press, an imprint of the
Crown Publishing Group, a division of Random House, Inc., New York.
www.crownpublishing.com

Three Rivers Press and the Tugboat design are registered trademarks of
Random House, Inc.

Previous editions of this work were published by Prima Publishing,
Roseville, California, in 1993, 1997, and 2000.

Library of Congress Cataloging-in-Publication data is available upon request.

ISBN 978-0-7704-3657-5
eISBN 978-0-7704-3658-2

Printed in the United States of America

Illustrations by Paula Gray and Adam DeVito
Cover photographs: Fuse/Getty Images

10 9 8 7 6 5 4

Fourth Edition

*To Alfred Adler and Rudolf Dreikurs for
their theories of mutual respect, and to the thousands of
school personnel and students who have confirmed
the value of these theories in schools.*

*A special thanks to those people who have
taken our ideas and used them in more creative ways
than we ever imagined.*

CONTENTS

CONTENTS

FOREWORD

A study conducted in the San Francisco Bay Area by the Lucille Packard Children's Hospital found that more than two-thirds of parents reported that their children experience moderate to high levels of stress as a result of their schooling and homework.* Another study found that when students were asked to choose one or two words to describe their experience in school, the most commonly chosen word was *bored*.† Our high school dropout rate is a national crisis, yet most students who choose to leave school are not failing but feel that school has no relevance to their lives. These are just a few of the

* Lucile Packard Foundation for Children's Health (2005). KidsData.org. Krackov, Andy, and Walsh, Eileen. New poll highlights parents' views on physical, emotional health of children.
† Lyons, L. (2004). Most teens associate school with boredom, fatigue. *The Gallup Youth Survey, January 22–March 9, 2004*. Retrieved June 24, 2009, from http://www.gallup.com/poll/11893/Most-Teens-Associate-School-Boredom-Fatigue.aspx.

many indicators that our children are disengaged and disenfranchised from school, leading to dire consequences for them, our communities, and our nation.

As a parent and school principal, I was introduced to Positive Discipline as a parenting program, but the more that I work with it and the more training our staff receives in it, the more I've come to see PD (as we like to refer to it) as an antidote for much of what ails education today. It's not a panacea, but it comes closer than anything else I know of to addressing the fundamental issue that lies at the heart of the crisis in education, and that is that our children have an almost complete lack of agency in their own schooling.

By "agency" I mean the belief that they can have an impact on what happens to them. Sadly, most students today feel that school is something that happens *to* them and not something in which they play a meaningful role. Sure, they're still called on to produce work and take tests, but rarely do they have any say in determining what that work is about or how they can best demonstrate understanding.

Positive Discipline is a philosophy that says that what children feel and think not only matters, it needs to be acknowledged, addressed, and incorporated into the regular structures of the school day for learning to be meaningful. Administered with fidelity, it's not just a stand-alone program in an antibullying effort, or a social-emotional learning curriculum, but a transformative vehicle for changing every aspect of education by affecting the tenets of the relationships that lie at the core of what we do when we teach children.

By involving children in making decisions about the things that affect them in the classroom, incorporating their suggestions into the class and school agreements, and utilizing their ideas as valuable resources in problem solving, both social and academic, we return to children a sense of agency and begin to transform their basic relationship with school. Our children can have as much of an impact on their school as the school has on them, and both the institution and the children will be better for it.

At Discovery Schools we believe in giving students choices about what and how they learn, but also in moving beyond choice to a partnership between teachers and students. Some of our seventh-grade students are currently designing their own progress reports as they learn about self-assessment, second graders are designing interest-based lessons to teach to their classmates, and our sixth graders just went on a field trip to San Francisco that was designed and planned entirely by the students. A tremendous amount of learning occurs in the logistical preparations for taking twenty-seven students on a trip out of town; it also builds responsibility, motivation, and relevance.

After our most recent PD in the Classroom Professional Development workshop, one of the teachers at our school made a list of the concepts and strategies that we were learning and practicing. It's an impressive list, including allowing natural consequences to be the teacher, being kind and firm at the same time, valuing mistakes as learning opportunities, guiding students but putting the onus for conflict resolution on them, and much more.

But the most impressive and important thing about *Positive Discipline in the Classroom* is the fundamental shift which is a trust in children, a belief that they bring unique skills and experiences to the table of their own learning, and that this is much more than just the place to start their growth of knowledge. It's a trust that they have wisdom of their own to impart, self-knowledge of how they learn best, the ability to self-assess both their learning and their behavior, and not just a right but a fundamental need to be critically involved in their own education.

Positive Discipline in the Classroom is all about creating the conditions to make this possible.

—*Dale Jones*
Executive Director, Discovery Charter Schools

POSITIVE DISCIPLINE

IN THE CLASSROOM

1

POSITIVE DISCIPLINE:
AN ENCOURAGEMENT MODEL

*A child needs encouragement like a plant needs water.
It is essential to healthy growth and development.*

RUDOLF DREIKURS

Many people think of academic study as the purpose of school and that discipline programs should support academic excellence. Therefore, adults administer common disciplinary approaches based on rewards and punishment in an effort to *control* students. However, research demonstrates that unless children are taught social and emotional skills, they have a tough time learning, and discipline problems increase.

Positive Discipline is a different approach. Picture a train trying to reach its destination on one track. It can't be done. The train needs two tracks, and so do our schools. The first track is academics, and the second track is social and emotional development. Positive Discipline consists of methods that involve students in focusing on solutions instead of being the recipients of punishments and rewards. Schools that have used this integrated system (both tracks side by side) report that behavior challenges decrease and academic excellence increases. The following photo, used with permission from the Visalia, California, School District, illustrates what they refer to as "A Climate for Learning."

A CLIMATE FOR LEARNING . . . TWO RAILS

Years ago one of the authors was struggling to learn how to use a computer—she wondered if it was worth all the effort. Then she heard someone say, "It's too late to decide whether there should be an *electronic train*. The choice now is when to jump on the train." His words have echoed in her mind as one new electronic development has followed another. Her world is filled with electronics that make her life easier and more interesting. She's glad she jumped on the train. Now that you've been introduced to the two tracks of Positive Discipline, we hope you'll want to jump on that train.

Before you shake your head and say, "No way! I can't handle one more thing in my already busy classroom," we hope you'll consider this: Positive Discipline will make your life easier. Really! If you're a kind and firm teacher who focuses on academics along with teaching social and emotional skills, you're already on board. If you're wondering if a Positive Discipline classroom is the direction you'd like to go, here are some questions for you to consider.

1. Do you want your students to be good decision makers?
2. Do you want your students to learn resilience?
3. Do you want your students to learn responsibility (response-ability)?
4. Do you want your students to learn cooperation?
5. Do you want your students to learn listening skills?
6. Do you want your students to learn to use self-control?
7. Do you want your students to learn to be comfortable with accountability?
8. Do you want to provide a forum where others can say how they were affected by hurtful behavior?
9. Do you want to help students learn how to make amends for the mistakes that hurt others?
10. Do you want a classroom where students are learning the qualities and strengths for good character?
11. Do you want a classroom where academic excellence can happen because students are encouraged to love learning?

Positive Discipline–trained teachers create classrooms where young people are treated with respect, have the courage and excitement to love learning, and have the opportunity to learn the skills they need for a successful life. The Positive Discipline vision is about schools where children never experience humiliation when they fail but instead feel empowered by the opportunity to learn from their mistakes in a safe environment. Many of the social and emotional skills students learn are represented in the Significant Seven Perceptions and Skills.*

Three Empowering Beliefs That Help Children Succeed in School and in Life

1. I am capable.
2. I contribute in meaningful ways, and I am genuinely needed.
3. I use my personal power to make choices that positively influence what happens to me and my community.

Four Empowering Skills That Help Children Succeed in School and in Life

1. I have discipline and self-control.
2. I can work respectfully with others.
3. I understand how my behavior affects others.
4. I can develop wisdom and judgment skills through daily practice.

Here is a description of how Positive Discipline methods teach the Significant Seven.

---

* On the Significant Seven, see H. Stephen Glenn and Jane Nelsen, *Raising Self-Reliant Children in a Self-Indulgent World* (New York: Three Rivers Press, 2002), which devotes a chapter to each component. It is also taught in the Developing Capable People Course. Go to www.positivediscipline.com for more information.

I AM CAPABLE

To develop a belief in their own personal capability, young people need a safe climate in which they can explore the consequences of their choices and behavior without judgments about success or failure— without blame, shame, or pain. Positive Discipline methods provide a safe climate in which students can examine their behavior, discover how it affects others, and engage in effective problem solving to create change.

I CONTRIBUTE IN MEANINGFUL WAYS, AND I AM GENUINELY NEEDED

To develop the belief in their significance in primary relationships, young people need the experience of having others listen to their feelings, thoughts, and ideas and take them seriously. They need to know "I am important, and I count." In a Positive Discipline classroom, everyone has the opportunity to voice opinions and make suggestions in an orderly, respectful process. Students learn that they can contribute significantly to the problem-solving process and can successfully follow through on chosen suggestions. They experience the primary goal of all people—a sense of belonging and significance.

I USE MY PERSONAL POWER TO MAKE CHOICES THAT POSITIVELY INFLUENCE WHAT HAPPENS TO ME AND MY COMMUNITY

Many teachers fail to understand that students have personal power and will use it in one way or another. If they are not given

POSITIVE DISCIPLINE IN ACTION

I can still remember the excitement I felt when I was first introduced to Positive Discipline because it seemed like just the thing I was looking for at that point in my teaching life. I found out about it through a student teacher who was with me for a whole year. We had a very challenging class. She left for a short time to do a "multicultural" unit at a troubled inner-city Seattle school. She called me shortly after she arrived to tell me about the amazing program that the principal had implemented. Apparently, it was the key that turned the place around. Guess what program that was?!

Long story short, I took a couple days off and went up there for a long weekend to talk to the principal, see how the program and Class Meetings worked in various grades, talk to teachers, observe students, etc. I was stunned to see how respectful the kids were and how inclusive the school felt. I came home with reams of materials and tons of ideas to use in my own classroom.

I absolutely loved the idea of Class Meetings, using the agenda, and giving kids a chance to really listen, brainstorm, and help solve problems within the room. My student teacher and I then shared what we were doing with other teachers in our school and were even asked to do a short presentation at another school in our district. Obviously, we weren't experts; however, our enthusiasm and positive results made up for that, I think!

Christine Hamilton,
Eugene, Oregon

opportunities to use it in productive ways, they will probably use it in destructive ways. Young people, to develop a healthy use of power in their lives, need the opportunity to contribute in useful ways, in an environment that encourages them but also holds them accountable. They need to learn to understand and accept their power to create a positive environment. A Positive Discipline classroom is a place where students can experience that it is okay to make mistakes and to learn from those mistakes. In Class Meetings, they learn to take responsibility for their mistakes (accountability), because instead of being punished, they receive assistance in exploring ways to learn from their mistakes. They also learn that even when they can't control what happens, they can control their response to what happens.

I HAVE SELF-DISCIPLINE AND SELF-CONTROL

A Positive Discipline classroom is an excellent place where students can name and claim their feelings and develop empathy and compassion. Young people seem to be more willing to listen when they are listened to. They gain understanding of their emotions and behaviors by hearing feedback from their classmates.  In a nonthreatening climate, young people are willing to be accountable for their actions. They learn what a feeling is and how to separate their feelings from their actions. They learn that what they feel (anger, for instance) is separate from what they do (hit someone), and that although feelings are always acceptable, some actions are not. Through the problem-solving process, they learn proactive rather than reactive ways to express or deal with their thoughts or feelings. They develop self-discipline and self-control by thinking through the consequences of their choices and by accepting suggestions for solutions from other students. The notion of inviting students to explore the consequences of their choices is quite different from imposing a consequence on them, which is usually a poorly disguised punishment. By exploring the consequences of choices, students learn from their mistakes instead of trying to hide them or defend them.

I CAN WORK RESPECTFULLY WITH OTHERS

A Positive Discipline classroom provides the best possible opportunity for young people to develop social skills through dialogue and shar-
ing, listening and empathizing, cooperating, negotiating, and resolving conflicts. When a behavior problem arises, teachers, instead of stepping in and resolving it for the students, can put it on the Class Meeting agenda, or use the Four Problem-Solving Steps, or instruct students in the use of the Wheel of Choice. All these methods, discussed in Chapter 7, allow students and teachers to work together on developing win-win solutions.

I UNDERSTAND HOW MY BEHAVIOR AFFECTS OTHERS

A Positive Discipline classroom is a place where students can respond to the limits and consequences of everyday life with responsibility, resilience, and integrity. They learn that it is safe to take responsibility for their mistakes because they will not experience blame, shame, or pain. They learn to give up the victim mentality of blaming others ("The teacher gave me an F") and accept an accountability mentality ("I received an F because I didn't do the work").

I CAN DEVELOP WISDOM AND JUDGMENT SKILLS THROUGH DAILY PRACTICE

Young people develop judgment skills only when they have opportunities to evaluate problems by being socially conscious and aware of what is happening around them. When a problem develops in a Positive Discipline classroom, students explore what happened, what caused it to happen, how their behavior affects others, and what they can do to prevent or solve such problems in the future. In this way, they learn to respond to the needs of the situation.

• • •

Students who are weak in the development of these three beliefs and four skills are at high risk for developing serious problems such as bullying, drug abuse, teen pregnancy, suicide, delinquency, and gang involvement. They are also at risk for developing less serious but very annoying beliefs such as a sense of entitlement and a lack of motivation. Students with strengths in the Significant Seven are at low risk for developing these serious and annoying problems. Obviously, it is extremely important that young people have the opportunity to learn the Significant Seven, and Positive Discipline provides an excellent opportunity to do so.

PUTTING IT ALL TOGETHER

Positive Discipline is effective when teachers are willing to give up control over students and instead work with them in a cooperative manner. Teachers who learn how to ask more questions and give fewer lectures develop a real curiosity about their students' thoughts and opinions. When students are encouraged to express their opinions, are given choices instead of edicts, and use group problem solving, the classroom atmosphere improves and becomes one of cooperation, collaboration, and mutual respect.

POSITIVE DISCIPLINE IN ACTION

My first year of teaching fifth grade was extremely hard. My way of dealing with challenging students was to simply get tough with them and demand that they shape up. Well, I'd get tough—but they'd get tougher. I'd get tougher, and they'd get even tougher! I finally realized that getting tougher was not the solution. Many of my fifth graders had siblings in gangs or parents in jail. I was not that tough! So what I really learned, that first year of teaching, was what did not work.

The next few years got a little better, but I still struggled with being too kind and then being downright mean. I would ask other teachers what they did in their classrooms *"to make kids follow directions."* One teacher whom I really respected told me that he drew a circle on the board and had the student stand with his or her nose to the circle! I decided I needed to figure this classroom management thing out on my own. I could never purposefully humiliate a child!

In my next few years of teaching, I figured out that being respectful and consistent with my students increased their willingness to be helpful. But I still struggled.

I then had the opportunity to take a Positive Discipline in the Classroom workshop. This workshop resonated with me in a *big* way! It was all about being respectful to students, growing their cooperation skills, giving them responsibility, letting them become problem solvers, and so much more! I felt so excited and energized. These were the skills that I wanted for my students (and for me)!

Teaching got better and better for me. I learned to create routines, jobs, and solutions *with* my students. We did Class Meetings every day—including compliments, appreciations, and problem solving. This process created a connectedness within the group that I had never experienced. The kids learned to trust each other, to help each other, and to care for each other. Overall, my students wanted to be positive leaders and strove to be their best selves. I finally felt like an effective and capable teacher!

I learned to become the leader and guide for my students instead of the controlling boss. My students learned that besides reading, writing, and math, they were skilled at communicating, problem solving, and working together. Those are important life skills!

One year, in the fall, a mother of a student from the previous year came to visit me. She wanted to thank me for all of the Class Meetings and problem solving we had done in class. Her son was attending a new school this year, with a teacher who was not being respectful to students. Her son went to the principal of his new school and asked if he could facilitate some Class Meetings to help the teacher and the students! Her son felt empowered to influence both his class and his new teacher. He wanted to make things better, not by blaming or finding fault but by simply discussing the problem and helping the students and teacher come up with a solution!

Dodie Bloomberg,
certified Positive Discipline lead trainer, Mesa, Arizona

2

POSITIVE DISCIPLINE:
A PARADIGM SHIFT

*An educator's most important task, one might say his holy
duty, is to see to it that no child is discouraged at school, and
that a child who enters school already discouraged regains his
self-confidence through his school and his teacher. This goes
hand in hand with the vocation of the educator, for education
is possible only with children who look hopefully and joyfully
upon the future.*

ALFRED ADLER

Imagine what it would be like to step into a world where everything
is different from the world in which you were raised. Perhaps you
grew up wanting to please adults. You worked hard for good grades
so your teachers and parents would be proud of you. You tried to be a
good child so you would avoid punishments. You became an approval
junkie. It did not occur to you that your thoughts and ideas should
matter to anyone.

Or you may have been one of those kids who fought the system.
You didn't care about rewards. You did your best to avoid punishments by not getting caught, but if you did, oh well. You became a

rebel. Sadly, you were more focused on rebelling against the thoughts of others than on examining your own thoughts.

Now—still imagining you are a child—you have entered a world where teachers don't use punishments and rewards. They want you to focus on solutions to problems—along with them. Instead of imposing consequences on you, they encourage you to think about the consequences of your behavior, and how it affects you and others. They believe that mistakes are opportunities to learn, and that sometimes you can choose to take some positive time out (in an area you helped create) to feel better before you are ready to learn.

How will you deal with this new world? Our guess is that it won't be easy to give up your dependence on or rebellion against adults who use extrinsic motivators (punishments and rewards) in favor of accepting responsibility and working with those who use intrinsic motivators (teachings skills for community and respectful problem solving).

This new world may not be any easier for teachers who are accustomed to discipline programs based on behaviorism. They too need a paradigm shift in their awareness. The following chart can help them explore the difference between two schools of thought.

TWO OPPOSING SCHOOLS OF THOUGHT ON HUMAN BEHAVIOR

Terry Chadsey and Jody McVittie, Certified Positive Discipline Trainers

	DOMINANT AND TRADITIONAL PRACTICE IN AMERICAN SCHOOLS	THE POSITIVE DISCIPLINE (SOLUTION FOCUSED) APPROACH
Who developed the theory?	Common practice, Pavlov, Thorndike, Skinner	Adler, Dreikurs, Glasser, Nelsen, Lott, Dinkmeyer
According to the theory, what motivates people's behavior?	They respond to rewards and punishments in their environment	People seek a sense of belonging (connection) and significance (meaning) in their social context

	DOMINANT AND TRADITIONAL PRACTICE IN AMERICAN SCHOOLS	THE POSITIVE DISCIPLINE (SOLUTION FOCUSED) APPROACH
When do we most influence the behavior of others?	At the moment when we response to a specific behavior	In an ongoing relationship founded on mutual respect
What are the most powerful tools for adults?	Rewards, incentives, and punishments	Empathy, understanding the beliefs of the student, collaborative problem solving, kind *and* firm follow through
What is the response to inappropriate behavior?	Censure, isolation, and punishment	Connecting before correcting, focusing on solutions, following through, and addressing the belief behind the behavior
What is the response to dangerous and destructive behavior?	Censure, isolation, and punishment	Ensure safety, followed by a plan for accountability and repair
How is student learning maximized?	When the adult has effective control over student behavior	When the student has learned social-emotional skills, developed self-control, feels connected to others, and makes contributions in the classroom

At the beginning of Positive Discipline workshops and classes, we help teachers increase their awareness of the need for change by asking them to create a list of what they want for their students—what kind of characteristics and life skills they hope their students will develop. For more than thirty years, in many different countries, hundreds of groups have created these lists, and they are all essentially the same:

Characteristics and Life Skills

- Healthy self-esteem
- Responsibility
- Self-discipline
- Cooperation
- Kindness
- Empathy

- Compassion
- Respect for self and others
- Problem-solving skill
- Sense of humor
- Resiliency
- Accountability
- Belief in personal capability
- Loving nature
- Honesty
- Lifelong learner
- Self-motivation
- Happiness
- Social consciousness

You'll notice that this list does not include academic excellence. We then ask the teachers how many think these characteristics and life skills are as important as academics. Every hand goes up. Then they say that these characteristics and life skills are even more important than academics because kids have to have these qualities in order to learn. Next, we ask teachers to brainstorm a list of behavior challenges. These lists are also very similar, regardless of the country from which they originate:

Behavior Challenges

- Not listening
- Talking back
- Lack of motivation
- Use of foul language
- Interrupting
- Homework problems
- Tardiness
- Sleeping in class
- Fighting
- Whining
- Temper tantrums
- Constant texting
- Media addiction
- Defiance
- Strong will
- Bullying

We go on to show the teachers how they can use the behavior challenges as an opportunity to teach the characteristics and life skills they want for their students. They learn this from their own experience by participating in a fun activity called Asking Versus Telling.

ACTIVITY: ASKING VERSUS TELLING

OBJECTIVE

To show teachers how to use behavior challenges as opportunities to teach the characteristics and life skills they want for their students

DIRECTIONS

1. Ask for a volunteer to role-play a student, then sixteen more volunteers to role-play teachers.

2. Divide the "teachers" into two lines, eight in each line. The "teachers" in one line of eight will have telling statements, and the other line will have asking statements.

3. Instruct the "student" to proceed down the line of "teachers" who have telling statements. The "student" stands in front of each "teacher" and listens to what he or she has to say without saying anything in response. The "student" just notices what he or she is thinking, feeling, and deciding.

TELLING STATEMENTS

1. You know you should have your books and homework ready before you come to class!

2. Don't forget to take your coat with you for recess, and be sure to put it on—it's cold outside!

3. If you don't get your work done in class, you'll stay in from recess and get it done then!

4. Put your papers away, books back on the shelf, and clean up before you leave the classroom!

5. Why can't you sit quietly like Sally?

6. Stop whining and complaining!

7. Okay! Who started this?

8. You just got a red card for talking.

4. After listening to these statements, the "student" is asked to share what he or she is thinking, feeling, and deciding. The "student" is then shown the list of Characteristics and Life Skills and is asked whether he or she is learning any of the qualities on the list. The answer is almost always no.

5. Next the "student" proceeds down the line of "teachers" with asking statements. He or she stands in front of each one and listens to what he or she has to say without saying anything in response—just noticing what he or she is thinking, feeling, and deciding.

ASKING STATEMENTS

1. What do you need to bring to be prepared for class?

2. What will you wear if you want to be warm outside at recess?

3. What is your plan for getting your work done before class is over?

4. What do you need to do to clean up your desk and classroom before you leave?

5. Who can show me how we sit when we are ready for the next lesson?

6. How can you speak to me so I can hear what you are saying?

7. How can you two solve this problem?

8. What was our agreement about not disturbing others during quiet time?

6. After listening to these statements, the "student" shares what he or she is thinking, feeling, and deciding. Teachers who listen closely learn that the asking statements are much more effective in helping students learn thinking skills and cooperation. The "student" is then shown the list of Characteristics and Life Skills again and is asked if he or she is learning any of those qualities. The answer is almost always "Most of them."

This activity illustrates the difference between behaviorism, where kids are told what to do (and receive rewards for compliance and punishment for noncompliance), and Positive Discipline, where kids are invited to think about what to do.

Why is it so much more effective to ask questions than to tell? Telling usually creates physiological resistance in the body. The message that is sent to the brain is *Resist*. By contrast, respectfully asking creates a physiological relaxation of the body, and the message that is sent to the brain is *Search for an answer*. The student feels respected, appreciates being involved, feels more capable, and usually decides to be cooperative.

FANTASY VERSUS REALITY

Many teachers fantasize about inspiring children to love learning. But too often that fantasy is hindered by the reality of discipline challenges. Years of research at reputable universities have shown that punishments and rewards are not effective for long-term behavior change,* yet administrators continue to try to help by introducing more discipline programs based on punishments and rewards. These programs may seem to help because they stop many discipline problems immediately. However, the long-term negative effects on kids are not considered.

To help explain this dilemma, we use the iceberg analogy of human behavior.

---

* Alfie Kohn, *Punished by Rewards: The Trouble with Gold Stars, Incentive Plans, A's, Praise, and Other Bribes* (Boston: Houghton Mifflin, 1993, 1999) cites hundreds of research studies (buried in academic journals) showing the long-term ineffectiveness of punishments and rewards. Kohn shows that while manipulating people with incentives seems to work in the short run, the strategy ultimately fails and even does lasting harm. Our workplaces and classrooms will continue to decline, he argues, until we shift away from our reliance on a theory of motivation that was derived from laboratory animals.

THE ICEBERG ANALOGY OF HUMAN BEHAVIOR

Many discipline programs address only the tip of the iceberg—the part you can see, the student's behavior. They attempt to manage behavior using punishments and rewards. Positive Discipline addresses the tip of the iceberg *and* the underwater portion.

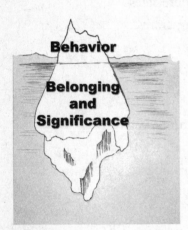

Psychologist Rudolf Dreikurs taught that children who misbehave are children who are discouraged. In other words, when children believe they don't belong, they "misbehave"— they choose a mistaken way to find belonging and significance. When teachers address only the behavior (the part they see), they do not deal with the discouragement that motivates the behavior. We call the part that is hidden under the surface the "belief behind the behavior."

It is understandable that teachers, like most adults, deal with what is on the surface. They've probably never thought of students as being like icebergs, and even if they have, they may not have the tools or knowledge to navigate around the underwater part of the iceberg. Teachers can easily be fooled into believing that the behavior is the issue instead of the belief behind the behavior. When teachers address the behavior only, they often create more discouragement, thus increasing misbehavior.

UNDERSTANDING THE UNDERWATER PART OF THE ICEBERG

Children continuously make subconscious decisions based on their perceptions, or private logic, of their life experiences. Some of these decisions are about themselves, such as "Am I good or bad, capable or incapable, significant or insignificant?" Others are decisions about other people: "Are others encouraging or discouraging, helpful or hurtful? Do they like me or dislike me?" Still others are decisions about the world: "Is the world safe or scary, nurturing or threatening, a place where I can thrive or a place where I need to try to survive?"

Children are not aware that they are making these decisions—centering on their need to belong and feel significant—but these decisions become their beliefs that affect their behavior.

When children feel safe—when they feel that they belong and are significant—they thrive. They develop into capable people with the characteristics and life skills teachers want them to have. When children believe they do not belong and are not significant, they adopt survival behavior. Survival behavior, often called misbehavior, is based on mistaken ideas about how to find belonging and significance. (We discuss this distinction more thoroughly in Chapter 4.)

We believe that the long-term result of using punishments and rewards to motivate behavior is discouragement. Children who like rewards soon depend on them for motivation and don't want to be contributing members of society for inner rewards—for feeling good about doing what is right even when no one is looking. The long-term results of punishment are described as follows:

Three R's of Punishment
1. **Rebellion:** "They can't make me. I'll do what I want."
2. **Revenge:** "I'll get even and hurt back, even if it hurts my future."
3. **Retreat:**
   a. Low self-esteem: "I must be a bad person."
   b. Sneaky: "I just won't get caught next time."

POSITIVE DISCIPLINE IN ACTION

I use Class Meeting time to help my fourth-grade students get to know each other and appreciate each other's positive qualities. To help them practice compliments and appreciation, at the beginning of the year during a Class Meeting, I draw one student's name from a bucket. Classmates brainstorm and name all the strengths and unique qualities of this one person, as I take notes. It is amazing how many positive and wonderful things students notice about each other.

I then take my Class Meeting notes and make a poster for each child, including all the positive qualities recorded and a picture of each child. These posters hang outside my fourth-grade classroom for the entire school to see. This process builds a sense of community and recognizes students for their unique qualities and contributions. Students have the opportunity to hear their classmates' and my positive perspectives about them—how encouraging! At midyear, after the posters have all hung together in the hallway for some time, these cherished posters are sent home for students to share with their family.

Mrs. Ohlin, a fourth-grade teacher,
Sandy Springs, Georgia

Since the three R's are the long-term results of punishment, why are so many programs based on a model that includes punishment, like the marbles in a jar in former years, or today's popular color-card system. Perhaps administrators and teachers who use punishment systems don't understand the long-term effects on students (based on the decisions they make about themselves) and their families. Maybe they are looking for something "simple" to stop problem behavior in its

POSITIVE DISCIPLINE IN ACTION

Today a four-year-old boy stormed away from the art table, screaming that he was "mad, frustrated, and not happy." My assistant followed him over to our comfy cushion, where he had wrapped himself in a blanket, now just screaming wordlessly and kicking the cushion. He refused to talk to the assistant, just continuing to scream. I sat next to him and whispered, "I need a hug." He continued screaming and writhing. After about fifteen seconds, I repeated, "I need a hug." He stopped screaming and flailing but kept his back to me. Ten more seconds. "I need a hug." Long pause. He turned over, climbed into my lap, and hugged me. I asked him if he wanted to go back to the art table by himself or if he wanted me to go with him. He asked me to go with him. He went back, finished his project happily, and left the table.

Steven Foster, L.C.S.W., early childhood specialist working with children with special needs, Positive Discipline lead trainer*

tracks. Maybe they think the system "works" because of short-term results.

The color-card system is one of those punishment-based programs that seem to get immediate results. However, several parents (and two teachers) shared their discouraging experiences with the color-card system on a Positive Discipline social network.

"My son started kindergarten yesterday," wrote a parent called

---

* Jane Nelsen, Steven Foster, and Arlene Raphael, *Positive Discipline for Children with Special Needs* (New York: Three Rivers Press, 2011), p. 55.

Lori, "and I need some advice. Both yesterday and today his teacher had the students come out one at a time to be released to their parents. I've noticed that the teacher is using this time as an opportunity to report on the child's behavior. She'll say things like 'She had a great day today—good job, Mom,' with a big smile on her face, or she'll list the 'offenses' that the child committed during the day. I was one of the lucky ones whose kid was released last, so I didn't have to be humiliated when she reported that 'he had a good morning, but he got a red card this afternoon.' Today I vowed that I would take my son by the hand, wave, and say goodbye before she had the chance to embarrass both of us in front of our peers. My son told on himself after school—he had a time-out because his card got moved to red. I asked him what happened and how he could avoid it tomorrow, and then we moved on with our afternoon.

"My husband and I are pretty upset, and he thinks I need to say something to the teacher. It really is so sad seeing the expressions on the faces of the kids *and* the parents alike—it breaks my heart because they just look crushed. While I can see my husband's point, I don't want to start off on the wrong foot with the teacher by inadvertently offending her. Which might happen if she thinks I'm attacking her approach as a teacher?

"Help! Should I say something, and if so, do you have any words of wisdom as to how I should approach her?"

A second parent reported this story: "My son is in third grade. He is constantly having to 'move his card' (that horrific color-coded behavior chart that so many teachers are using these days) and is made to sit alone—away from his classmates, or he has recess taken away.

"Last week he was sent to the principal's office three times! Once for interrupting seven times while the teacher was teaching a lesson (attention-seeking from peers), once for coloring on a table and not stopping after being asked, and a third time for rolling his eyes at the teacher. I'm just so tired of hearing all the negative comments from teachers. When he gets in trouble at school, I'm supposed to take away video games and other privileges at home. I don't want to do this, but my husband thinks we should—so we fight about it and both feel like terrible parents. Someone asked if the color-card system has helped my son. Of course it hasn't."

Two teachers weighed in on the color-card system.

"As a teacher," wrote Jennifer, "I always like to hear parents' points of view so I can improve my own classroom management. I'm fortunate enough to work in a school that has done away with cards this upcoming year. Yeah! From a PD standpoint, I did not like to use them. Plus I found them bothersome during class and would forget to use the system at all. I certainly can't speak for all teachers, but I would not be offended if parents approached me with their concerns. I would be embarrassed that I didn't realize how this might affect them and their children. I am sure the intention is good."

"Like Jennifer, I am a teacher," wrote Heather. "I teach first grade and have used Positive Discipline for years, but a large majority of the other teachers at my school do not. The card system/clip system is a favorite of many of them, and like so many PD folks here, I just think it's awful. I could go on and on about this topic *forever*, but I guess I wanted to share how wonderful it is that many parents are aware of how detrimental the card system can be, as well as a teacher who publicly humiliates a student's behavior, and that they are willing to speak up.

"Out of all the teachers at my school who use the card system, I really can't think of one who wouldn't at least be open to hearing a parent's concerns. If you present them in a respectful way (and maybe throw in some of those great Curiosity Questions), hopefully your child's teacher will really hear you. Maybe add something like "I know how much you care about your students, and knowing that you've only known my child for a few days, I'm sure you weren't aware of how anxious s/he feels when it's time to leave for school."

We do not believe children should "get away" with unacceptable behavior. This book is filled with nonpunitive and nonrewarding tools to teach children socially acceptable behavior. And just as it takes time for children to learn academic skills, it takes time for children to learn social skills.

Think about what it takes for a child to learn to talk—years of example, first to say a word, then more listening to examples and encouragement to learn sentences, and more years to keep developing and perfecting language. Why do we expect immediate results for other kinds of learning? And how well would children learn to talk if they were humiliated and punished every time they got it wrong? Children learn what they live. If we want our children to grow up learning to be kind and firm and respectful, we must make sure that that is what they live.

Let's time-travel forward. The following story comes from Lynn Lott, coauthor of this book and a psychotherapist, who tells us about a sixteen-year-old girl who got in trouble back when she was in kindergarten.

"Yesterday I worked with a sixteen-year-old who was referred to me because she's had severe stomach problems for over a year with no medical origin. We did some childhood memory work to extrapolate her core beliefs that were created during her early years. The first memory she had was of kindergarten, where she was corrected four times for talking in class and told to sit in the Thinking Chair, a humiliating and embarrassing situation even at age five.

"After being punished at school (first punishment), her parents were called in for a conference, and the teacher explained that their daughter (an only child) would not be allowed to be in the kindergarten play because she talked too much (second punishment). When the child got

POSITIVE DISCIPLINE IN ACTION

This happened today in my social skills class for preschoolers. Ryan was having an awful morning, hitting kids repeatedly, telling adults to shut up, running off, etc. Near the end of the day I pulled him aside and described his day. I told him it looked like he was having a very hard day. Kids were mad at him. He was telling grown-ups to shut up. Predictably he told me to shut up...again. I asked him whether something happened at home that was bothering him.

"Shut up!"

I said that I really wanted to help him but didn't know what to do.

"Shut up!"

I asked him if he wanted a hug.

"No!"

I said. "Hmm. You're feeling pretty icky and you don't want a hug. You know what? I could use a hug. Will you give me one?"

Long stare. I say nothing.

He launches himself at me and squeezes.

"Wow, that's a nice hug! I could use another one like that."

He gives me another one.

We go have a snack. His life still is in chaos. But his last ten minutes of class go smoothly.

Powerful.

It seems that asking for hugs is helpful even in nontantrum moments.

Steven Foster, L.C.S.W.

home, her parents lectured her and punished her by taking away toys (third punishment).

"She decided to play it safe and try to stay out of trouble. Her version of staying out of trouble was and is to stay low on the radar, including getting mediocre grades so she doesn't stand out. It made her nervous when she got A's and B's, so she figured out how to get B's and C's so no one would expect much of her. She stopped caring about school or thinking it was important. Unfortunately, this decision leaves her sick to her stomach—literally."

The excessive use of punishment is not unlike a form of abuse. If parents and teachers knew they were going to create lifetime problems from their punitive approach, they most likely would look for alternatives. They simply do not understand or consider the long-term results of their methods.

This book is filled with alternatives. If we were to choose just one alternative to the color-card system, it would be to ask a student who is behaving improperly, "How can we solve this problem?" This does not leave children feeling humiliated. Instead it helps them feel capable and teaches them to focus on solutions to mistakes. For many variations on the theme of solutions, see Chapter 7.

3

LEADERSHIP STYLES

*We can change our whole life and the attitude of people
around us simply by changing ourselves.*

RUDOLF DREIKURS

One of the sad aspects of teaching is that too often teachers never see the fruits of their labor. They plant the seeds but don't experience the harvest. But in a Positive Discipline classroom, the teacher does not have to do all the labor and planting alone, and the benefits of a kind and firm leadership style are obvious almost immediately.

Responsible citizenship requires a high degree of social interest—the desire and ability to contribute in socially useful ways. In a Positive Discipline classroom, students solve problems together and learn the tools of mutual respect, cooperation, and collaboration. They experience the positive use of power, and this empowerment reduces their need to act out and create problems in order to feel powerful.

The accompanying story exemplifies an early harvest from students learning responsible citizenship.

POSITIVE DISCIPLINE IN ACTION

Let there be no doubt that our students are learning to have a voice, to problem-solve, and to collaborate! I have a story to share that brought me to tears. Class meetings are an integral part of the Positive Discipline approach, similar to family meetings within the home, and all our students have Class Meetings on a regular basis.

Our fourth graders this year learned how to conduct their own classroom meetings, where they are in charge of the agenda and problem-solving steps. A few weeks ago a teacher shared with me that several of our fourth graders had conducted their own meeting during lunchtime, and they were discussing forming a group and holding their own elections. A week or so later another teacher shared with me that the fourth graders wanted to make posters to show their support of the Libyan people and the injustice they are facing these days.

Then a couple of fourth-grade students came into the office and asked to meet with me to discuss a group they had formed together—and looking at my schedule and theirs, we chose to meet during recess yesterday. When I arrived at work in the morning, I found an e-mail, from the nine-year-old who founded the group, letting me know more about the organization and its goals. Here's an excerpt from that e-mail:

"I have noticed that Earth is getting harsher and harsher. I want to change the world with the help of children, because I want kids to realize that they can do the impossible, and make it possible. This is why I have founded KCCW (Kids Can Change the World). You must be younger than eighteen to be recruited (unless you worked as a part of KCCW when you were a kid but you are now an adult). I want you to do me a small favor; tell everyone you know about KCCW. The goals of KCCW are:

- End poverty
- End war
- End pollution
- Save endangered animals
- Promote education
- End drugs
- Freedom for all

"KCCW motto 'Make the world a better place.' "

Thinking I would be meeting with just a few students, I was overwhelmed that almost the entire fourth-grade class showed up in my office. These students were clearly committed to KCCW, and the group was gaining members! KCCW is an example of what can happen when you believe students are capable and act in ways to support your belief in their capabilities. These students truly believe they can make the world a better place, and I believe they can too! This is a wonderful example of the type of leadership and empowerment that New Horizon is fostering in our children. How would these students have ever achieved the belief that they can change the world in a school without Positive Discipline?

Dina Eletreby, head of New Horizon Elementary School,
a Positive Discipline school in Irvine, California

LEADERSHIP STYLES

Classroom atmosphere is established from the top. When a teacher's kindness involves rewards, and when firmness involves punishment, children can become confused and fearful of the judgments about their worthiness: "Am I a good boy/girl, or a bad girl/boy in this moment?" But when teachers are kind and firm at the same time, they help children become responsible, reliable, resilient, resourceful, empowered, capable, caring, and self-assured.

One child shared with her grandma that she got a yellow card in school. Her grandma asked her what it meant. "Oh, it means that I'm just a little bit bad," the little girl said. Of course her grandma was horrified to think that her precious granddaughter was deciding she was even a little bit bad instead of understanding that she made a poor behavioral choice.

Too many adults expect children to develop wisdom and sound judgment without practicing, making mistakes, learning, and trying again. Positive Discipline classrooms give young people a great deal of practice time. A foundation of mutual respect and student involvement is imperative. The combination of kindness and firmness is encouraging and usually helps a student experience a sense of belonging and significance—and thus improved behavior.

Are you kind and firm at the same time? If not, check out the following three leadership styles and see if they describe you. It's important to know yourself and your leadership style so you can decide what and if you'd like to change.

Leadership styles that may be popular but don't lead to empowered, socially conscious kids are called the Boss, the Rug, and the Ghost.

The Boss believes, "It's my way or the highway. I'll tell you how to behave and what to do, and you'd better do what I say, or you're in trouble."

The Rug believes, "I'm here to make you happy and comfortable. You tell me what you want and need, and I'll make it happen."

The Ghost is an absent leader who disappears (emotionally if not physically), hopes for the best, and is off doing something else.

These leaders may use punishments and rewards as their discipline system. Punishment assumes that children need to pay for what they have done or failed to do. In other words, "In order to make children *do* better, first we have to make them feel worse." This approach often leads to feelings of resentment, revenge, rebellion, and retreat. Rewards assume that children will to do what we want only when they receive external rewards. This approach negates the inner good feelings that come from contributing, and often leads to demand for bigger and better rewards.

POSITIVE DISCIPLINE FOR BEHAVIORAL CHANGE

Positive Discipline teachers look for opportunities to help children learn from their experiences. Allowing natural consequences is actually a discipline choice. Natural consequences occur without any adult intervention. If a child forgets her raincoat and it rains, she will get wet. If a child cuts in line, another classmate will probably say, "No cuts." If a child forgets his or her lunch, fifteen classmates (excuse the sarcasm) will probably offer to share what they have, especially the parts their parents packed that they don't like. Many issues in a classroom are easily and quickly solved without any adult interference. If you are feeling uncomfortable sitting back, at least count to ten in your head and see what happens before you jump in thinking you have to micromanage the situation.

KIND AND FIRM LEADERS TEACH THAT MISTAKES ARE OPPORTUNITIES TO LEARN

Teachers have many opportunities to help students change misguided notions about mistakes. Many of your students play video or computer games, so it may be helpful to talk about mistakes in this context. When children make a mistake on a video game, they simply try again. It may take one hundred tries to figure out how to solve a problem or get to the next level. The video game doesn't scold or shame players; it's set up to keep them trying and to encourage them to learn from past errors. Life isn't all that different. Every person in the world will continue to make mistakes as long as he or she lives.

Hiding mistakes keeps people isolated. Mistakes that are hidden can't be fixed; nor can people learn from them. Good judgment comes from experience, and experience comes from poor judgment.

Because we all make mistakes, it's healthier to see mistakes as opportunities to learn instead of statements of inadequacy. When the whole class really understands that they can learn by making mistakes, individual students will not mind being accountable for their own. They'll see it as an opportunity to get valuable help from their classmates. They'll actually learn to be proud to take responsibility for what they've done, even if it was a mistake, because they know it doesn't mean they're bad or will get in trouble. One way to teach that mistakes are wonderful opportunities to learn is by having everyone in the class share a mistake they made and what they learned from it. Another way is through the following activity.

ACTIVITY: MISTAKES ARE WONDERFUL OPPORTUNITIES TO LEARN

OBJECTIVES

To help teachers be aware of their own unhealthy concepts about mistakes

To teach students healthy concepts about mistakes

DIRECTIONS

1. Think back to your childhood and your life as a student (or ask students to think about their experiences now). Remember the messages, both stated and implied, that you heard about mistakes. Write them down. Following are some typical messages:

- Mistakes are bad.
- You shouldn't make mistakes.
- You are stupid, bad, inadequate, or a failure if you make mistakes.
- If you make a mistake, don't let anyone find out. If someone does, make up an excuse even if it isn't true.

2. Based on these messages, what decisions did you make about yourself or about what to do when you made a mistake? Some typical decisions:

- I'm bad when I make mistakes.
- People will think less of me if I make a mistake.
- If I make a mistake, I should try not to get caught.
- It's better to make excuses and blame others than to accept responsibility.
- I'd better not take a risk if I know I can't do something right or perfect.

3. Explain that all these decisions are "crazy notions" about mistakes. Talk with students about people they know who have made mistakes and then dug themselves into a hole trying to cover them up. Then discuss how forgiving people can be when others admit their mistakes, apologize, and try to solve the problem they have created.

KIND AND FIRM LEADERS USE ENCOURAGEMENT INSTEAD OF PRAISE AND REWARDS

Encouragement is the foundation of every concept discussed in this book. Encouragement tells students that what they do is separate from who they are, and it lets them know that they are valued for their uniqueness without judgment.

Ask yourself what you would say to a student who got A's and B's on his report card. You might say, "You're doing so well. You must feel very good about that. You're really smart." What would you say if that same student earned only D's and F's? He still needs supportive feedback, but it will be much harder for you to think of positive things to say. Following are some examples.:

How do you feel about your grades?

What happened? Do you have any idea why your grades are dropping?

Would you like some help improving your grades? I'd be happy to help you with your spelling words.

Hey, anyone can have a bad report card. We still like you a lot.

I bet you're feeling scared to show this to your parents.

Here's an activity on encouragement that you could use with your students or at a teachers' meeting.

ACTIVITY: ENCOURAGEMENT TO GO*

OBJECTIVES

To help students anticipate that they might feel discouraged at times, even after they acquire new skills

To make a contribution to someone else

MATERIALS

Index cards

Pens or pencils

A bag or a hat for the index cards

DIRECTIONS

1. Hand out an index card to each student.

2. Give the students examples of things that might shake their confidence:
   - You tried something and it didn't work.
   - You got upset and couldn't stop yourself from yelling or being mean.
   - Someone criticized or made fun of you when you were trying.

3. Tell the students you would like them to write on their index card words of encouragement *they* might like to hear when their confidence is shaken. If they can't compose sentences yet, have them dictate to someone who can, or draw pictures. Give examples to the students such as "I know you'll figure it out," or "Hang in there—you can do it," or "Want a hand? I can help if you like."

---

*This original activity was developed by Elizabeth Dannhorn and Steven Foster and has been revised for classroom use by Lynn Lott and Jane Nelsen.

4. As they write, tell the group that each of them will be leaving class today with a piece of encouragement from someone else.

5. Walk around the circle and collect the cards in the bag or hat. Make sure to thank each student.

6. Proceed with the class.

7. Before dismissal, ask each student to pick a card from the hat or bag and take it with them when they leave.

KIND AND FIRM LEADERS CREATE ROUTINES WITH THE HELP OF THEIR STUDENTS

Routines establish a sense of order and stability. Life is easier for everyone when the day's events have a smooth rhythm. A routine is something students can learn to count on. The routine itself becomes the "boss," so teachers or students don't dictate what will happen. It's more empowering for students to hear "Who can tell me what's next on our routine chart?" than to hear "I need you to do your spelling now." The first statement implies that the teacher is asking students to check the routine and see what needs to be done, while the second suggests that the teacher should be controlling. Many students feel rebellious when told what to do, but they'll gladly do what needs to be done when they've been respectfully involved in the process.

Most teachers build a lot of routines into their classes. We suggest you look for places where you can involve the students in setting up routines. For maximum success, use limited choices. Ask students whether they prefer to do math or English first, or whether they'd like to have their art period before lunch or at the end of the day.

Setting up routines works especially well for scheduling class job times, deciding how materials will be distributed and collected, establishing the way students enter and leave a room or line up for recess in elementary school, and following procedures outside the classroom (such as assemblies, field trips, and fire drills). You can create routines that are predictable, consistent, and respectful by following these Five Guidelines for Setting Up Routines. Use them while working with your students during Class Meetings.

Five Guidelines for Setting Up Routines

1. Focus on one issue at a time. Example: "First we'll work on making a job chart. After we've used it for a week, we'll decide if it's working well. If it isn't, then we can figure out a better way to collect and hand out papers."

2. Discuss the issue when everyone is calm rather than during a time of conflict. Example: If you notice that a routine isn't working well, write yourself a note or put the item on the Class Meeting agenda. When everyone is calm or at a Class Meeting, ask for help with improving the routine. If you try to fix it in the middle of chaos, it can be very difficult.

3. Use visuals, such as charts and lists. After students agree on the order in which things will be done, you or one of your students can make a chart itemizing the routines. When it's time for reading, ask your students, "What's next on our schedule?" The schedule becomes the boss instead of the teacher.

4. Rehearse by role-playing. Have the class pretend that it's time for the chosen activity, and go through a practice run so that everyone knows what's expected.

5. Once a routine is established, follow it faithfully. If a student questions or ignores an established routine, ask, "Could you check

the routine chart and let me know what's next?" Resist reminders and nagging. Let kids make mistakes, then send them to the routine chart to see what the routine is set up to be.

Establishing routines yields long-range benefits of security, a calmer atmosphere, and trust. Routines also help students develop life skills. Students learn to be responsible for their own behavior, to feel capable, and to cooperate in the classroom.

HOLD PARENT-TEACHER-STUDENT CONFERENCES

We advocate that you eliminate parent-teacher conferences and instead hold parent-teacher-student conferences. Many teachers have told us they already do this. They recognize the importance of involving students in any process that directly affects them. Because the purpose of parent-teacher conferences is to encourage students, doesn't it make sense that the student should be present? Don't we teach "It's not polite to talk about people behind their back"?

To ensure that a parent-teacher-student conference will be an encouraging process, prepare in advance. Create an Encouragement Form using the following questions.

1. What is going well?
2. What is needed to encourage and support what is going well?
3. In what areas would improvement be beneficial?
4. What is needed to support improvement?

List the student's name, the teacher's name, and the parent's name at the top of the form. Give one copy of the Encouragement Form to the student and one to the parent, and keep one for yourself. Ask that each person complete the form before the parent-teacher-student conference. With children who can't write their answers by themselves, let them dictate to you or an aide.

At the conference, go over each item on the list. Ask the student to share what is going well first. Then each person at the conference can add his or her appreciation for what is going well. Brainstorm together what is needed to encourage and support continued success.

Next, allow the student to share first in the areas of needed improvement. Students know where they need to improve, and having them go first increases accountability instead of the defensiveness they might feel if the adults went first. However, it is important for everyone at the meeting to share his or her perceptions. Again, everyone can brainstorm ways to encourage and support improvement. Let the student choose which suggestions would be most helpful. When the student and adults disagree about what needs  improvement, allow everyone a turn to share his or her reasons while the others listen. It's possible that parents and teachers have goals that the student does not share. Until goals are shared, the student will defeat any efforts for improvement.

Adults might benefit from the point of view expressed in the book *Soar with Your Strengths*. It begins with a delightful parable about a duck, a fish, an eagle, an owl, a squirrel, and a rabbit that all attend a school with a curriculum that includes running, swimming, tree climbing, jumping, and flying. All the animals have strength in at least one of these areas but are doomed to failure in others. It hits close to home to read about the punishment and discouragement that these animals encounter when parents and school personnel insist they must do well in every area in order to graduate and become well-rounded animals. A major point of the book is that "excellence can be achieved only by focusing on strengths and managing weaknesses, not through the elimination of weakness."*

Teach students to manage their weaknesses and soar with their strengths. Parents, teachers, and students can all work together to help each other soar. That is what people do when they feel encouraged.

WHAT ANIMAL ARE YOU?† SELF-AWARENESS IS A KEY TO KIND AND FIRM LEADERSHIP

Here's another way to think about what kind of leader you are and how your personality influences your work in the classroom. Are you a chameleon, a turtle, or an eagle? To find out, answer the following question:

> Which would you most want to avoid dealing with: pain and stress, rejection and hassles, meaninglessness and unimportance, criticism and ridicule?

It helps to read those words out loud, noticing if you have an uncomfortable reaction to hearing one set over another.

PAIN AND STRESS If you chose pain and stress, you're a turtle teacher. As a leader, you can be creative, diplomatic, easygoing, and permissive or spoiling with students. When you're stressed, you've got

---

* Donald O. Clifton and Paula Nelson, *Soar with Your Strengths* (New York: Dell, 1992). See also Jane Nelsen, Roslyn Duffy, Linda Escobar, Kate Ortolano, and Debbie Owen-Sohocki, *Positive Discipline: A Teacher's A–Z Guide* (Rocklin, Calif.: Prima, 1996), p. 61.
† Based on an activity called "Top Card" in the *Teaching Parenting the Positive Discipline Way Manual* by Lynn Lott and Jane Nelsen, pp. 251–256.

that lovely turtle shell to curl up in. Or if things get too crazy, you can become a snapping turtle, scaring everyone away until you feel safe. Want a leadership challenge? We have three for you: set up routines, communicate with others, and allow kids to experience the consequences of their choices.

REJECTION AND HASSLES   If you chose rejection and hassles, that makes you a chameleon teacher. Your leadership style is to be tuned in to others. You're friendly and giving but easily hurt. Sometimes you let yourself be a doormat or take everything personally. You love being loved by your students, so you have to be careful that you don't let things get out of hand or do things to meet your need for approval rather than your need for order. When you are stressed, you need to work on setting boundaries, doing joint problem solving, and saying how you *really* feel instead of giving in too much. Watch out for gossiping or saying yes when you mean no.

MEANINGLESSNESS AND UNIMPORTANCE   Those of you who chose meaninglessness and unimportance are lion teachers. You are knowledgeable learners; you take the initiative and have high ideals. Unfortunately, you can burn yourself out or underestimate others' abilities. You might push others as hard as you push yourself, thinking that things can always be better. In the classroom, we suggest you work on giving up your need to be right and concentrate on trusting others and having patience. In the spirit of giving others good advice, you sometimes come across as arrogant or critical, which isn't your intention. We've known some lion teachers who roar pretty loudly or bite off someone's head when they feel threatened. That's not you, is it?

CRITICISM AND RIDICULE   Finally, if you chose criticism and ridicule, you're the eagle. That makes you an advance planner who likes to be in charge. You might be superorganized or superscattered, procrastinating with the best. It's tough for you to delegate. You like to be the helpful one who takes care of things. When you're stressed, you have a tendency to withdraw to your nest, which can scare your students, because they can feel abandoned. When you think you've been criticized, you can turn from an easygoing, predictable teacher into a screaming, attacking bird of prey. Want to work on your leadership style? How about saying how you feel, delegating, and giving people choices?

If you find this section on leadership helpful and interesting and want to learn more, you can find an interactive chart with more information at Lynn Lott's Web site, www.lynnlott.com.

THE CONTINUUM OF CHANGE

Many teachers are accustomed to directing students, and many students are used to being directed by teachers. Ineffective habits are easier to break when you replace them with empowering ones. Expect some reluctance as you begin the process of helping students develop the capacity to solve their own problems. Students who have never had to take responsibility (because teachers have taken it all, through punishments and rewards) may not be thrilled with the idea in the beginning. Once they experience the dignity, respect, and self-satisfaction that come from being a capable contributor to their environment, however, they will rise to the occasion.

Understand that students will find it difficult to change their behavior until teachers change theirs. To help students learn self-control, self-discipline, responsibility, and problem-solving skills, don't hesitate to take the lead.

Kind and firm leaders are realistic about change. Change is a process involving awareness and skill development, practice and time. Think about learning to ride a bicycle. Most of you didn't jump onto a two-wheeler and ride it down the street on your first try. In the beginning, you were probably unconsciously unskilled, thinking, *I could do that.* Once you got on the bike, you became consciously unskilled, thinking, *I'll never learn how to ride that thing.* With the help of training wheels or someone running alongside you, you began to get the hang of pedaling, but you were also screaming, *Don't let go! Don't let go!* As you practiced more with the help of those wheels or an adult, you became more skilled and eventually became consciously skilled, thinking, *I'm doing it, I'm doing it.* At some point, the training wheels were taken off or the person running by your side let go, and you realized you could do it, even though you may have been very wobbly or even fallen over a time or two. Once you mastered the process, you became unconsciously skilled, riding your bike with ease. Even if you didn't ride for several years, you told yourself, *Riding a bike is something you never forget!*

What does all this have to do with kind and firm leadership? We think switching to Positive Discipline develops the same way. As a teacher, in the beginning you might be thinking, *This is a no-brainer. I can do it.* That's the unconsciously unskilled part.

Once you try to figure out where to begin, it may all seem too hard and too complicated. Don't stop here—that's just the consciously unskilled part. With some "training wheels" and practice, you'll feel more confident to try out new tools, even though you're still thinking about everything you do and maybe even falling flat at times. Now you're consciously skilled. One day you'll look back on making the change to Positive Discipline and wonder if there was ever a time you didn't lead this way. Now you're unconsciously skilled.

It's the same for the students. Change is challenging and takes time and encouragement. Most kids come from homes where the leadership style is vertical, where the parents are boss and dole out punishments for behaviors they don't like. Or they micromanage their children incessantly. Such children aren't used to thinking for themselves or taking responsibility for their behavior. Under the leadership of a kind and firm teacher, they can make the transition, but it won't happen overnight. Still, the results are worth the effort. If you provide some good training at the beginning of the school year and maintain some patience and faith that kids can become unconsciously skilled, the rest of the year will be much easier on everyone.

USE TEACHERS HELPING TEACHERS PROBLEM-SOLVING STEPS

Have you ever noticed how easy it is to solve someone else's problem? The reason is obvious. We can bring objectivity and perspective to the problems of others when we're not emotionally involved.

But challenging students often push buttons that cause teachers to react instead of act. These students need more understanding and more encouragement than the average student does—and so does the teacher who is required to meet the challenge.

When you're facing a discipline problem, your school may have a referral procedure, and you may be expected to seek out administrators or counseling staff to handle it. We are suggesting that before you do so, you try following the Teachers Helping Teachers Problem-Solving Steps on page 48. You may end up with an encouraging change that will influence the student in a positive way. Many teachers find that using these fourteen steps gives them ideas for encouraging students and turning around their behavior. Both teachers and students feel empowered by the process, and school referrals diminish significantly.

The Teachers Helping Teachers Problem-Solving Steps can be used with a group of teachers who take turns being the facilitator, the volunteer who presents a challenge, and being a participant who volunteers for role-playing and brainstorming for solutions. However, you might want to use the steps with one or two friends (one of whom will volunteer to present a challenge). If you work in a school that is using the Teachers Helping Teachers Problem-Solving Steps with the entire faculty, you could practice with one or two friends before facilitating this process with a larger group.

The steps will take you to an action plan that will invite children to do and feel better. That doesn't imply that the volunteer presenting the challenge is the problem, but it does consider the powerful notion that if the teacher changes what he or she does a little, it will change what kids do a lot.

The trick is to *follow the steps exactly and trust the process.* As the facilitator, you will read the steps (presented on the following pages) out loud, pausing to give the "volunteer" a chance to respond briefly to each question. Be sure to have a copy of the Mistaken Goals Chart on page 58. (You'll see where it is needed in Step Nos. 5 and 6.) You don't need to write anything down other than the information from Steps 2 and 3, and the brainstorming suggestions in Step No. 10.

Hold a copy of these steps in your lap and cover up the steps with a blank sheet of paper. Uncover one step at a time and read it so that the volunteer can respond to the information. There is never any need to memorize these steps. Reading them helps you stick to the steps. Do not analyze or add information that isn't in the steps. That's right—*no analyzing*!

Teachers Helping Teachers Problem-Solving Steps

1. Thank the "volunteer" for being a co-teacher in this process because everyone will learn from what is shared.

2. Write the following information on flipchart paper. (While practicing it can be on a sheet of paper.) What grade level are you teaching? Make up a name (confidentiality) of the challenging student (or students). How old is the student?

3. Give a one-word or one-sentence headline of the problem.

4. Describe the last time the problem occurred. Use enough detail and dialogue (like a movie script) so that you and others will be able to role-play the situation in a later step. If the volunteer needs help describing the situation, you can ask, "What did you do?" "What did the student do?" "Then what happened?" "What happened next?"

5. "How did you feel?" If the volunteer has difficulty expressing a one-word feeling, refer to the second column of the Mistaken Goals Chart (on page 58) so he or she can choose the group of feelings that fit.

6. Based on the feeling expressed, use the Mistaken Goals Chart to guess the student's mistaken goal. (It is not important to guess correctly. New information may come out in the role-play. Guessing gives you a working hypothesis.)

7. Would you be willing to try something else that would be more effective?

8. As best as you can, given that there may be only two of you, set up and perform a role-play of the scene that was described. Remember that the role-play can be as brief as one minute to give all the information needed. If you have extra people helping, they can role-play, too. It is usually best for the person presenting the problem to role-play the child—to "get into the child's world."

9. After the role-play, each of you share what you were thinking, feeling, and deciding (to do) as the person you played.

10. Together, brainstorm possible solutions the volunteer could try. Write down every suggestion. (When done in a larger group, the volunteer gets to sit in a "cone of silence" while listening to others brainstorm for possible solutions.)

11. Ask the volunteer to choose a suggestion he or she would be willing to try for one week.

12. Role-play the chosen suggestion for practice. Ask the volunteer if he or she would like to practice doing the chosen suggestion, or role-play the child to see what it feels like from the child's perspective. Process each role-player as you did in Step 9 for thoughts, feelings, and decisions.

13. Will you commit to try the suggestion for one week and to share the result at the end of the week?

14. Give volunteer appreciations for the work done, which might include what you (as a participant) learned from it.

Typical Problems When Using the Problem-Solving Steps

1. You don't follow the outline or stick to the steps.

2. You get caught up in the story. It's important to stick to one time when the problem occurred. Background information is not necessary for this process.

3. You analyze, question, and evaluate information.

4. You don't think about suggesting some of the tools you've learned as you've read this book or tools that can be found in the last column of the Mistaken Goals Chart.

5. You skip steps, such as role-playing or appreciations. Every step is important, even if it's just two of you using them.

The Teachers Helping Teachers Problem-Solving Steps serve as intake, assessment, diagnostic tool, treatment plan, action plan, and encouragement process all rolled into one. The steps are effective because they give teachers practical ideas and skills that work for positive change. Going through the steps with other teachers is not only fun and nonthreatening, it also eliminates the endless analysis that often focuses on causes, blame, and excuses instead of helpful action.

Even teachers who have been reluctant to try the Teachers Helping Teachers Problem-Solving Steps have been impressed by the encouragement and help they received through this process. They've been surprised at how much understanding they gained by role-playing the student (or others) to "get inside their shoes." They have enjoyed the encouragement from their colleagues and have acquired many ideas they can use to encourage their students. (And yes, these steps work for any relationship issue whether at home, work, or at school.)

A seventh-grade teacher tried the steps with another teacher at lunchtime. She was reluctant to do so at first, thinking there were too many. Like many teachers, she thought this would make more work for her instead of less. Here is what happened:

> *What we liked was that after explaining the situation that was happening, we got to express how it made us feel. After we did all fourteen steps, we talked about how it was different from what we usually did—i.e., complain. Anyhow, what we really liked was that we were able to express what we were feeling, which made the whole thing worthwhile in our minds, and altered the severity of the student interaction once we saw how we were playing into it. We want our whole school to use it! Thank you.*

OTHER SUGGESTIONS FOR KEEPING YOURSELF ENCOURAGED

While you are making the shift to kind and firm leadership, you need to find ways to stay encouraged, especially if you are odd man out in your school. If you can find or create a group of like-minded teachers who meet regularly as a mentor group, that's the best. If you can't, you can stay in touch with other PD educators at www .positivediscipline.ning.com, a friendly community where parents and teachers support and encourage each other in the use of Positive Discipline.

If you haven't attended a two-day Positive Discipline Workshop, you can find a schedule at www.positivediscipline.com and at www .positivediscipline.org. The Positive Discipline Association offers thorough training in the Teachers Helping Teachers Problem-Solving Steps at its two-day Positive Discipline in the Classroom workshops. You could also invite a Positive Discipline facilitator to bring a two-day workshop to your school.

When we were first learning about Positive Discipline, one way we both stayed encouraged was to teach others what we ourselves wanted to learn. With every parenting and teacher training class we taught, we moved forward on the continuum of change. We invite you to teach what you want to learn using the myriad Positive Discipline books and manuals that are available. If you're the kind of person who wants to be trained before you train others, the Positive Discipline Association has many programs to become a certified Positive Discipline trainer.

POSITIVE DISCIPLINE IN ACTION

Upon my arrival at Roosevelt Elementary as principal, I found that its discipline plan focused on external rewards and punishment,* little cards that were given to reward students for good behavior. (If a child did anything good, he or she expected a card.) These cards were put in a pot, ten cards were pulled weekly, and a prize was given. On the last day of school an awards assembly was held, with about twenty cards pulled out for larger prizes from a garbage can full of cards. Consequences took the form of removal from the classroom, in and out of school suspensions, and spending time in "the center." An educational assistant staffed the center. She helped students who had been removed from the classroom do schoolwork and write apology letters or scripts of the broken rule and what they should have done. There were scripts for virtually every occasion.

During the first month of school, I went into the center during recess and found eighteen students packed in the little room, which ideally accommodated no more than ten. When I questioned them, very few knew why they had been sent there or how long they would be removed from their classes. That was the day I realized that Roosevelt's student intervention program should change. I also knew it would not be easy, as the center was the only thing the teachers told me should remain the same when I became principal thirty days before.

It took me one year with the old discipline policy to create a climate that recognized the need for change. We held a day-and-a-half training to learn how to implement Positive Discipline. During the training

---

* The name of this five-hundred-student elementary school has been changed and the principal has asked to remain anonymous. Thirty percent of the school's students qualify for free and reduced lunch.

I wish I could say every teacher was on board and that there was an immediate transformation, but that is not true. As I looked at the faces of teachers, I knew some were participating half-heartedly; however, the experiential lessons moved some teachers from being unwilling to being willing to try it out. My hardcore teachers, who did not see the need for change, did not change that first year.

But I have seen most resisters gradually adopt therapeutic time-out or "Hawaii," Peace Table, and our Wheel of Choice [see Chapter 7] because it is more effective. Classroom meetings are now the norm at Roosevelt. Although again there are pockets of resistance, most teachers have classroom meetings and marvel at the improved classroom climate. As the principal, every day I see situations that show me that Positive Discipline is making a huge difference in the ability of our children to communicate their feelings, use strategies to solve interpersonal problems, and be more empathic to the problems of others. I also believe this strategic thinking is helping them in their schoolwork.

Today I had several experiences that showed me the power of Positive Discipline. I was in the lunchroom, and a little girl came up to me and said, "I gave George three 'I' statements, and he still will not stop bugging me." Last year this little girl (I will call her Mary) would have retaliated by knocking this boy off his lunch bench. It was interesting to me that her real problem and outrage stemmed not from the irritating actions but from the fact that he was not listening to her even after three "I" statements. When I spoke with the boy, his defense was that Mary offered only one "I" statement and he most certainly would have responded to three. He quickly said he would stop the behavior and that he "didn't really hear her the first time." Both of these third graders would have escalated into a verbal or physical fight two years ago.

Another change is our parents. Our school counselor works with parents individually to help them resolve communication problems with their children. At the last PTSA meeting, she presented some Positive Discipline concepts, which included the Mistaken Goals Chart. This was the most attended PTSA meeting we had all year, with several couples attending. Later in the year a parent said she thought Positive Discipline was extremely important to her children and one of the best things about Roosevelt.

Cultures do not manifest complete change overnight or even over two years, but at Roosevelt the process has begun. Now our community of students, teachers, and parents work to act in a respectful manner for a more effective academic environment. We now have the knowledge and skills to interact with each other in a way that supports one another, thereby achieving a win/win situation. Before Positive Discipline at Roosevelt, respect was just a word; now it is actions.

WHY PEOPLE DO WHAT THEY DO

Meanings are not determined by situations, but we determine ourselves by the meanings we give to situations.

ALFRED ADLER

Discouragement is at the root of all misbehavior.

RUDOLF DREIKURS

A misbehaving student is a discouraged student. When students believe they don't belong, they usually choose one of the Four Mistaken Goals of Behavior:

Undue Attention
Misguided Power
Revenge
Assumed Inadequacy

When you are faced with misbehavior in your classroom, it's only natural for you to deal with the tip of the iceberg (the behavior) before you know about mistaken goals (the underwater part of the iceberg). Olive is waving her hand, jumping up and down, calling, "Teacher, teacher!" What's your natural inclination? Do you give her attention by

saying her name, correcting her, and maybe even giving a short history lesson like this: "Olive, how many times have I told you to wait your turn? If I've told you once, I've told you a thousand times. Put your hand down and wait until the other student is finished talking." You can say this a hundred more times, but Olive will continue her annoying behavior. Why? Because she thinks she is important only when she gets constant attention.

Then there's Nate, pushing and shoving in line to be first. When he's at the playground, he's taking the ball away from the other students so he can have it. He defies you constantly in class, being oppositional and stubborn. Again, what would be your natural reaction to this tip-of-the-iceberg behavior? Most teachers (and parents too) would fight back, showing Nate that he can't be the boss. Nate believes on some unconscious level that he has to win and be in control to belong, so he will fight the adults' attempts to control him to the bitter end.

Peter comes to school in dirty clothes and picks fights with others. The kids don't like him or want to sit by him because he's mean. He's

been known to steal other kids' school supplies and then lie, saying he has no idea who took Ryan's new pencil. It's easy to react to Peter's behavior with barely hidden disgust, to try to lecture him into compliance and let him know just how unacceptable his behavior is. But Peter's behavior is just the tip of the iceberg. Underneath, he feels hurt, unloved, disliked, and not good enough, and he believes he has to get even by hurting anyone who comes into his path.

Finally, there's little Lilly, who gives up before she starts anything. No matter how much coaxing you do, she won't try. She does the

best she can to make herself invisible until you stop asking anything of her. She will likely end up labeled with a learning disability, but that's simply dealing with the tip of the iceberg. Underneath, she is convinced that no matter what she does, it won't be good enough, so why should she bother trying? She will work overtime to be left alone and train students and teachers not to expect anything of her.

The Mistaken Goals Chart will help you understand the underwater part of the iceberg—the discouraging beliefs that fuel a behavior.

The mistaken goals were identified by Rudolf Dreikurs. When he was once asked, "How can you put children in these boxes?" he replied, "I don't put them there, I find them there." The Mistaken Goals Chart will help you identify mistaken goals in your students and suggest encouragement ideas to help change the beliefs. Many teachers keep a copy of this chart on their desks as a quick reference when faced with a behavior challenge.

Here's how to use the Mistaken Goals Chart. Think back to Olive, Nate, Peter, and Lilly. Do you have students in your class who act as they do? Look at column two: which of the feelings listed there are closest to what yours would be? Your feelings are your first clue to let you know the *child's* mistaken goal. Look at column three: what do you usually do in response to the child's behavior? Does the student react as described in column four? This is your second clue to verify the *child's* mistaken goal. These first four columns show you what is happening in the tip of the iceberg.

Column five explains the underwater portion of the iceberg, the part you can't see. It's the child's mistaken understanding of how to belong and feel significant. The sixth column shows you that when children are "misbehaving," they are speaking in code. Adults can be more

MISTAKEN GOALS CHART

THE CHILD'S GOAL IS:	IF THE PARENT/ TEACHER FEELS:	AND TENDS TO REACT BY:	AND IF THE CHILD'S RESPONSE IS:	THE BELIEF BEHIND THE CHILD'S BEHAVIOR IS:	CODED MESSAGES	PARENT/TEACHER PROACTIVE AND *ENCOURAGING* RESPONSES INCLUDE:
Undue Attention (to keep others busy or to get special service)	Annoyed Irritated Worried Guilty	Reminding. Coaxing. Doing things for the child he/she could do for him-/ herself.	Stops temporarily, but later resumes same or another disturbing behavior	I count (belong) only when I'm being noticed or getting special service. I'm important only when I'm keeping you busy with me.	*Notice Me Involve Me Usefully*	Redirect by involving child in a useful task to gain attention. Say what you will do. (Example: I love you and will spend time with you later.") Avoid special service. Have faith in child to deal with feelings (don't fix or rescue). Plan special time. Help child create routine charts. Engage child in problem solving. Use family/class meetings. Set up nonverbal signals. Ignore behavior with hand on shoulder.
Misguided Power (to be boss)	Challenged Threatened Defeated	Fighting. Giving in. Thinking, *"You can't get away with it or I'll make you."* Wanting to be right.	Intensifies behavior. Complies with defiance. Feels he/ she's won when parent/ teacher is upset even if he/she has to comply. Passive power (says yes but doesn't follow through).	I belong only when I'm boss, in control, or proving no one can boss me. You can't make me.	*Let Me Help Give Me Choices*	Redirect to positive power by asking for help. Offer limited choices. Don't fight and don't give in. Withdraw from conflict. Be firm and kind. Don't talk—act. Decide what you will do. Let routines be the boss. Leave and calm down. Develop mutual respect. Set a few reasonable limits. Practice kind and firm follow-through. Use family/ class meetings.
Revenge (to get even)	Hurt Disappointed Disbelieving Disgusted	Hurting back. Shaming. Thinking, *"How could you do such a thing?"*	Retaliates. Intensifies. Escalates the same behavior or chooses another weapon.	I don't think I belong so I'll hurt others as I feel hurt. I can't be liked or loved.	*I'm Hurting Validate My Feelings*	Acknowledge hurt feelings. Avoid feeling hurt. Avoid punishment and retaliation. Build trust. Use reflective listening. Share your feelings. Make amends. Show you care. Encourage strengths. Don't take sides. Use family/class meetings.

MISTAKEN GOALS CHART (*CONT'D*)

THE CHILD'S GOAL IS:	IF THE PARENT/ TEACHER FEELS:	AND TENDS TO REACT BY:	AND IF THE CHILD'S RESPONSE IS:	THE BELIEF BEHIND THE CHILD'S BEHAVIOR IS:	CODED MESSAGES	PARENT/TEACHER PROACTIVE AND *ENCOURAGING* RESPONSES INCLUDE:
Assumed Inadequacy (to give up and be left alone)	Despair Hopeless Helpless Inadequate	Giving up. Doing things for the child that he/she could do for him-/herself. Overhelping.	Retreats further. Becomes passive. Shows no improvement. Is not responsive.	I can't belong because I'm not perfect, so I'll convince others not to expect anything of me. I am helpless and unable. It's no use trying because I won't do it right.	*Don't Give Up On Me Show Me a Small Step*	Break task down into small steps. Stop all criticism. Encourage any positive attempt. Have faith in child's abilities. Focus on assets. Don't pity. Don't give up. Set up opportunities for success. Teach skills—show how, but don't do for. Enjoy the child. Build on his/her interests. Use family/class meetings.

effective when they learn how to break the code instead of the child. Column six helps teachers break the code by understanding what a child is really saying with the coded message. The last column provides specific encouraging and empowering interventions that teachers can make.

SAME BEHAVIORS, DIFFERENT GOALS

Some behaviors may fit under every mistaken goal. Not doing homework is a good example. When a child's failure to do homework invites you to feel annoyed or worried, the child's mistaken goal is Undue Attention. When this behavior invites you to feel challenged or defeated, the child's mistaken goal is Misguided Power. When this behavior invites you to feel hurt or disappointed, the child's mistaken goal is Revenge. When this behavior invites you to feel hopeless or inadequate, the child's mistaken goal is Assumed Inadequacy.

THE ICEBERG JUNGLE

The Iceberg Jungle is an activity that we do in workshops. It helps teachers understand the Mistaken Goals Chart, identify the long-term effects of punishment, and learn how to replace discouraging statements with encouraging and empowering ones. Many teachers with whom we work prefer to be encouraging, but they can't always think of the words that would encourage. To help them, we have created a list of sentences of encouragement that can be used for each specific mistaken goal as well as a list of sentences that would work for any of the mistaken goals.

We encourage you to get a group of teachers together and do the activity for maximum understanding. We've found that teachers learn much more and retain it much longer when they experience an activity instead of simply reading about it.

ACTIVITY: THE ICEBERG JUNGLE

OBJECTIVES

To help teachers identify the long-term effects of punishment

To help teachers replace discouraging statements with encouraging and empowering ones

DIRECTIONS

1. Divide the teachers into four groups, each consisting of four to six. Each group works on one of the Four Mistaken Goals in the Mistaken Goals Chart.

2. The groups take one of the four following posters, corresponding to its mistaken goal.

3. Give the teachers in the four groups some sticky notes. Ask them to write down behaviors that invite them to feel the feelings in column two for the goal they represent. The teachers paste those sticky notes on the tip of the iceberg.

4. The teachers in the Undue Attention group choose one person to play a student. The rest of them stand on chairs, lined up in a row, to play "teachers." The "student" holds the poster in front of his or her chest and walks along the line and pauses in front of each teacher.

5. The "teachers" on the chairs respond reactively to the behaviors on the sticky notes with exaggerated actions and/or statements from the third column of the Mistaken Goals Chart. The "student" does not react but just listens to the discouraging (but familiar) statements and notices what he or she is thinking, feeling, and deciding.

6. At the end of this role-play, the "student" shares what he or she was thinking, feeling, and deciding while listening to the teachers. Usually, the "student" says something like "I was thinking these teachers are mean (or stupid). I was feeling angry (or hurt), and I was deciding to avoid them and just rebel (or give up)." We also ask the "teachers" what they were thinking, feeling, and deciding while they were being so discouraging. Many of them admit that they know that what they are doing is not effective. They just don't know what else to do.

7. Show the "student" the list of Characteristics and Life Skills (on page 15) and ask if he or she has learned anything from this list. The answer is always no.

8. The "teachers" get down off the chairs and are given slips of paper, each with one or more of the Encouraging Statements. The "student" again

walks down the line and pauses in front of each "teacher" and listens as the "teacher" reads aloud an Encouraging Statement.

9. Afterward the "student" is asked what he or she was thinking, feeling, and deciding when these statements were read, and what he or she has learned, referring to the list of Characteristics and Life Skills. Usually, the reply is, "Most of them." The teachers are also invited to share what they were thinking, feeling, and deciding. Many are surprised that they didn't realize how much more effective they feel when using Encouraging Statements.

10. The groups representing the other Mistaken Goals repeat the process.

Encouraging Statements for Undue Attention

Let's make a deal. How about if you sit down and get some work done and we can hang out for a few minutes at recess.

That's important. Please put it on the agenda.

I hear you, but I can't answer that until recess.

Would you be willing to hand out these papers?

That doesn't work with me. If you'd like, I'm happy to talk it over respectfully when you're ready.

This is quiet time. We can talk out loud later.

I care about you, and the answer is no.

Please save that thought for special time.

Tomorrow you can take a whole minute to lead the group in making funny faces.

Ask me later.

Encouraging Statements for Misguided Power

What is your understanding of our agreement?

What was our deal?

I need your help. What ideas do you have to fix this problem?

Let's negotiate. Why don't you tell me what you have in mind and I'll tell you what I have in mind, and we can see if there's something that could work for both of us.

What would help you the most—to put this problem on the agenda or find a solution on the Wheel of Choice (see Chapter 7)?

Instead of arguing, do you want to put this on our Class Meeting agenda, or should I?

That's one way. I look at it differently. Want to hear what I think?

We can listen to each other without agreeing.

I think we are in a power struggle. Let's take some time to calm down and then start over.

We'll do it this way until we have time to work out a plan we all like.

Encouraging Statements for Revenge

You're really feeling hurt. I'm so sorry.

Why don't we both take a break, cool off, and then come back and try again.

I'm not interested in who started this. I'd like to know how we can work it out respectfully.

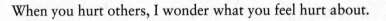

You must be upset because you always get in trouble and _____ walks away without getting caught.

Let's walk to the playground together.

When you hurt others, I wonder what you feel hurt about.

Looks like you are having a really bad day. Want to talk about it?

Do you know I really care about you?

We can work this out, but not this way.

Encouraging Statements for Assumed Inadequacy

Remember when you first tried to _____? Remember how long it took until you were good at it?

How about doing this small step first?

Let's do it together.

Your brain gets stronger by trying new things and doing them over and over.

It's okay to make mistakes. That's how we learn.

Your smile lights up our room.

I'll write the first letter, and you write the next one.

I can't remember how to _____. Could you show me? I could really use some help.

Encouraging Statements for Any Mistaken Goal

Would you be willing to work with me to figure out whether you'd like to improve your grade, and if so, how you could go about that?

When you've put away the equipment, we can move on to the next activity.

Let's try it this way for a week, and then we can reevaluate.

You can try again.

I'll let you know when I'm ready to try again.

I wonder what you're so upset, angry, hurt, annoyed, etc. about.

Wow! You're really angry, upset, annoyed, etc. Want to tell me about it?

I feel _____ because _____ and I wish _____.

Pencil. Quiet. Later. Recess. (One word!)

I can tell this is really important to you.

I can see how hard you worked on this and how much time went into it.

As you read the Iceberg Jungle Activity and the Encouraging Statements, you can probably think of many places where you could use them. You might want to make multiple copies of the statements and put them where they are easily accessible so you can refer to them when you know encouragement is needed but you can't remember the words. These statements can be modified to use at home or at work or with loved ones.

You can also teach your students about the Four Mistaken Goals. Teachers who have taught their students how to use the Mistaken Goals Chart to recognize discouraged behaviors, and find options that actually work, say this is one of the most powerful tools for peaceful classrooms.

It can be very encouraging for children to have a better understanding of the beliefs behind behavior and of the fact that "misbehaving people are discouraged people." The following activity will teach students how to use their brainstorming skills to encourage each other.

ACTIVITY: FOUR MISTAKEN GOALS

OBJECTIVES

To give students tools to encourage each other in ways that can make a difference

To help students with difficult behaviors find belonging and significance in the classroom without having to act out—to be proactive instead of reactive.

MATERIAL

A laminated Mistaken Goals Chart, enlarged enough for everyone to see

DIRECTIONS

1. Hang the Mistaken Goals Chart in a prominent spot and ask your students to think of a situation in which they felt irritated. Point to "Irritated" in column two. Run your finger across the chart to the last column to show the students the list of possible encouraging responses that they could use when they feel irritated. Go to column five, which is the belief behind the child's behavior. Tell your students that if they feel irritated, the person they have a problem with may think, *I count (belong) only when I'm being noticed or getting special service. I'm important only when I'm keeping you busy with me.*

2. Put your finger on the first column, and let your students know that the child's mistaken goal is called Undue Attention.

3. Emphasize that if a student wants to help a person change his or her irritating behavior, all he or she has to do is use encouraging solutions from the far right side of the chart.

4. Repeat the same exercise with each of the mistaken goals. That is, ask for a situation in which they felt angry (Misguided Power), hurt (Revenge), or hopeless (Assumed Inadequacy). Go through the chart for each of these feelings as you did for Undue Attention.

5. Point out that if students simply react instead of understanding about discouragement and offering more encouraging choices, all that will happen is the "misbehavior" will continue.

COMMENT

The powerful message to students is that they can change their behavior to be encouraging and that that might invite the other person to change. The Mistaken Goals Chart gives suggestions that invite misbehaving kids to act in a more respectful, encouraged, and empowered way.

Once students understand how to identify the mistaken goals of other people, encourage them to use their skills in class. The following chart was created by students in a fifth-grade classroom to illustrate how they could be encouraging to kids in each mistaken goal.

ENCOURAGEMENT CHART

UNDUE ATTENTION	MISGUIDED POWER	REVENGE	ASSUMED INADEQUACY
Walk with them to school.	Ask for their ideas.	Tell them you're sorry if you hurt their feelings.	Let them help someone else with something they are good at.
Sit by them at lunch.	Let them be a line leader.	Be their friend.	Tell them they are okay.
Laugh at their stories.	Put them in charge of a project or chore.	Invite them to your birthday party.	Have another student work with them.
Talk to them.	Ask for their help to tutor another student.	Compliment them.	Tell them math was hard for you, too.

One class made signs to put on the ends of craft sticks for each of the mistaken goals. Each student had a set of four sticks. The class agreed that if anyone behaved in a disruptive way, students would guess what the mistaken belief might be and hold up the appropriate sign. The intent was not to label, blame, or stereotype, but rather to offer a friendly reminder for the disruptive person. The misbehaving student could then decide if he or she would like to choose contributing behavior instead of disruptive behavior.

There is an amusing footnote to this story. Guess who got the Misguided Power sign most often? The teacher. This good-natured teacher would say, "Okay, I see that I'm trying to boss you around. Who has ideas about what I could do to invite cooperation?" This teacher modeled that it is not bad to make a mistake and that the group can help each other make effective changes.

Two of our colleagues came up with songs to help parents and teachers understand the Four Mistaken Goals better.* Playing the Mistaken Goals songs can enhance students' understanding of them. After each song ask, with a sense of fun, if any of the behaviors mentioned in the song sounded familiar. You can also watch for recognition reflexes (laughter, grins, head nodding) while the songs are being played. Lead a discussion on what students think about the mistaken belief in each song and their suggestions about how people in the songs could be encouraged.

Here's how a high school principal dealt with the underwater part of iceberg behavior. The first time principal Jim Sporleder tried an encouraging approach to student discipline at Lincoln High School in Walla Walla, Washington, he was surprised that it worked. In fact, it worked so well that he never went back to the old behaviorist approach to student discipline. A news article reported what happened.

A student blows up at a teacher, drops the F-bomb. The usual approach at Lincoln—and, safe to say, at most high schools in

---

* Wayne Frieden and Marie Hartwell-Walker, *Behavior Songs,* audiotape (Orem, Utah: Empowering People Books, Tapes, and Videos, 1988). For information, call 1-800-456-7770.

this country—is automatic suspension. Instead, Sporleder sits the kid down and says quietly:

"Wow. Are you okay? This doesn't sound like you. What's going on?" He gets even more specific: "You really looked stressed. On a scale of 1–10, where are you with your anger?"

The kid was ready. Ready, man! For an anger blast to his face . . . "How could you do that?" "What's wrong with you?" . . . and for the big boot out of school. But he was not ready for kindness. The armor-plated defenses melt like ice under a blowtorch and the words pour out: "My dad's an alcoholic. He's promised me things my whole life and never keeps those promises." The waterfall of words that go deep into his home life, which is no piece of breeze, end with this sentence: "I shouldn't have blown up at the teacher." *

According to the article, the kid apologized to his teacher without being told. He was also sent to in-school suspension, which in Sporleder's school is a positive time-out space where kids can calm down, catch up on homework, or talk about anything with the supervising teacher. The article compared the number of suspensions before the new approach of asking kids what's going on (798) to the number after Sporleder's changes were instituted (135).

We challenge you to take an hour, a half-day, a day, or even a week and dedicate yourself to exploring the underwater of the iceberg of your students. We would love to have you share your success stories on the Positive Discipline Facebook page or in our blogs.

---

* "Lincoln High School in Walla Walla, WA, Tries New Approach to School Discipline—Suspensions Drop by 85%" *ACES Too High News,* April 23, 2012, http://acestoohigh .com/2012/04/23/lincoln-high-school-in-walla-walla-wa-tries-new-approach-to-school -discipline-expulsions-drop-85/. See also "Walla Walla: A Compassionate Approach to Discipline," *League of Education Voters,* June 26, 2012, http://www.educationvoters .org/walla-walla/.

POSITIVE DISCIPLINE IN ACTION

A child began music class yesterday just fine. But in the middle of a discussion about "The Blue Sky Song," she suddenly announced, "I am a dog!" She lay down in the middle of the circle and began barking. I kindly asked her to please sit up and listen, but she didn't, nor did she make eye contact with me.

I noticed my emotion—*irritation*—and thought about the Mistaken Goals Chart in the Positive Discipline model. What do I do with this child? Redirect? Suggest she take a break? I thought about a task she could do for me there in the music room. It took me a minute, but I decided to try asking her to take all the xylophones off the shelves for me. Xylophones were not the next activity, but we would be playing them at the end of class. Without addressing her "barking" at all, I whispered to her, "Would you please help me by taking the xylophones out?"

She immediately stopped barking and went quietly to work. The rest of the class and I finished our discussion. At the end, she contributed to the discussion with some wise and interesting words. Then we sang two songs, played a game, and did the xylophone activity. She was polite and concentrated throughout and turned out to be quite a good musician (which I told her).

So, hurray!!! No unpleasant scene!!! I have no idea why she acts out, but it's so wonderful that the Positive Discipline strategies work as well as they do.

Music teacher, Aurora School,
Oakland, California

5

CONNECTION BEFORE CORRECTION

To see with the eyes of another, to hear with the ears of another, to feel with the heart of another. For the time being, this seems to me an admissible definition of what we call social feeling.

ALFRED ADLER

Strong scientific evidence demonstrates that increased student connection to school predicts school success. It decreases absenteeism, fighting, bullying, and vandalism while promoting educational motivation, classroom engagement, academic performance, school attendance, and completion rates. Connection is the belief on the part of students that adults in the school care about their learning and about them as individuals. In other words, in order to succeed, students need to feel they "belong" in their school. These seven qualities seem to influence students' positive attachment to their school:

- Having a sense of belonging and being part of a school
- Liking school
- Perceiving that teachers are supportive and caring
- Having good friends within school
- Being engaged in their own current and future academic progress
- Believing that discipline is fair and effective
- Participating in extracurricular activities

These seven factors, measured in different ways, are highly predictive of success in school because each brings with it a sense of connection—to oneself, one's community, or one's friends.* Even though the research is impressive, even more convincing are reports from students.

A group of middle school students were asked, "What usually happens when you get in trouble at school?" The kids responded with various answers, including detention, Saturday school, lunch detention, suspension, extra homework, getting yelled at, being grounded or beaten at home, having parents come to school and sit with them to embarrass them, or referral (which they defined as getting sent to the office to listen to a speech).

The students were then asked, "How many of you have experienced any of these consequences?" Two out of ten had been beaten at home for poor behavior in school. Five had had their parents come to school. Everyone had served detention, been grounded, been yelled at, or received extra homework. At least seven out of ten had received lunch detention, Saturday school, and suspension. When asked if these

---

* "School Connectedness: Strengthening Health and Education Outcomes for Teenagers," special issue of *Journal of School Health* 74, no. 4 (September 2004), http://www.jhsph .edu/departments/population-family-and-reproductive-health/_archive/wingspread /September issue.pdf.

interventions helped them do better in school, they said "No!" in unison. When asked if the interventions helped them feel loved, cared for, and motivated to cooperate, they laughed and replied, "What do you think?"

"Why do you think grown-ups do these kinds of things if they don't help?" we continued. "Because they like the power," some answered. "You don't think they do it because they care about you and want to help you do better?" we asked. The kids just laughed.

CREATING A CONNECTION

Students' belief that teachers care about them is a primary ingredient for their feeling a sense of connection (belonging and significance). Dr. James Tunney, a former educator and National Football League referee, did a study for his doctoral dissertation to measure levels of perceived caring.* He first surveyed principals with the question "Do you care about your teachers?" The principals always reported high levels of caring. Dr. Tunney then surveyed the teachers and found that they perceived extremely low levels of caring from their principals.

The next step was to ask the teachers, "Do you care about your students?" Of course, the teachers reported high levels of caring about the students. But guess what? The students perceived extremely low levels of caring from their teachers.

During in-service training, when we ask teachers how many of them care about kids, just about every hand goes up. Then we ask, "How

---

* James Joseph Tunney and James Mancel Jenkins, *A Comparison of Climate as Perceived by Selected Students, Faculty and Administrators in PASCL, Innovative and Other High Schools* (Ph.D. diss., University of Southern California, 1975).

many of you think your students know you care?" Although fewer hands are raised, most teachers still believe students are getting the message. Unfortunately, as Dr. Tunney's research shows, very few students believe that teachers care about them unless they are getting good grades. They tend to believe teachers care only about A students who have "psyched out" the teacher and who know how to play the teacher's game.

The following activity could be done during a faculty meeting to give teachers a platform for sharing ways to demonstrate caring.

ACTIVITY: DO THEY KNOW YOU CARE?

OBJECTIVE

To provide a reality check on how often and in what ways teachers send the message of caring to their students

COMMENT

Research has shown that the greatest predictor of achievement is the student's perception of the question "Does the teacher like me?"

MATERIALS

Butcher paper

Marking pens

Masking tape

DIRECTIONS

1. With a group of teachers, discuss the doctoral dissertation study done by Jim Tunney, described previously.

2. Form groups of three to five people. Each group gets a large piece of butcher paper and a marking pen.

3. Each group chooses a person to act as the recorder. In three minutes, they brainstorm as many ways as possible to show students they care. The recorder writes down every idea.

4. At the end of three minutes, the groups hang their papers on the wall with masking tape. A volunteer from each group reads the lists.

5. Process the activity by discussing:

What insights did you gain?
What do you notice about your behavior with students? What goals are you setting for next week about how to show students you care?

6. Have a volunteer type a list of all the ideas from all the groups, eliminating duplicate ideas. Distribute copies to each teacher to use as a reminder of things to do each day to demonstrate caring to students.

One group of teachers who did this activity identified that students know you care when you find out who they are, encourage them to see mistakes as opportunities to learn and grow, and have faith in their ability to make a meaningful contribution. They know you care when they feel that you listen to them and that you take their thoughts and feelings seriously. They know you care when you respect them enough to involve them in decision-making processes. They know you care when you help them understand the consequences of their choices in a nonthreatening environment that encourages problem solving instead of punishment.

THE POWER OF CARING

An atmosphere of caring begins when the teacher guides students to treat one another in ways that demonstrate caring. Carter Bayton, a teacher in an inner-city New York school, expressed the idea of caring in these moving words: "You have to reach the heart before you can reach the head." In September 1991 *Life* magazine featured a story about Bayton and seventeen second graders who had been labeled "unteachable" in a regular classroom.* Bayton taught the unteachables so well that in six months they challenged the "regular" class, which they had been deemed unfit to enter, to a math contest—and won!

Carter Bayton understands the importance of treating students with kindness and firmness. He understands that making sure the message of caring gets through is a truly essential part of the teacher-student relationship. Teachers have many opportunities to convey a message of caring. We encourage you to seize them. When students feel cared about, they want to cooperate, not misbehave. When they do not need to misbehave to gain attention and significance, they are free to learn. More hints on ways to show caring can be found in the following barriers and builders.

CONNECTION ATTITUDES AND SKILLS

As we've seen, many teachers do care about their students, but the kids aren't getting the message. Even though you may feel strongly about connecting with students, you could be doing some things that send a different message, as did a teacher in a junior high school class. The students were in serious conflict with this teacher, who couldn't understand their hostility. A visitor to the classroom observed the teacher's manner and heard her tone of voice. (This teacher, like many,

---

* Denise L. Stitson, "Yearning to Learn," *Life*, September 1991.

was unaware of her tone and how it affected the students.) Whenever students misbehaved, she yelled at them, criticized them, and humiliated them in front of their classmates. After class the shocked visitor asked the teacher if she would like some feedback. She said yes and was told, "You are trying to put out a small fire with a blowtorch." Now aware of her manner and tone, the teacher changed both by the next class period. That same day she told another faculty member, "My classes have been much smoother this afternoon, since I decided to put away my blowtorch."

At the end of an experiential activity during a Positive Discipline in the Classroom workshop, one teacher was amazed to realize that "When I criticize my students, I say it loud enough for others to hear. When I have something nice to say, it is in a soft voice that others usually don't hear."

LISTEN AND TAKE KIDS SERIOUSLY

Robert Rasmussen, called Ras by his students, was voted High School Teacher of the Year five years in a row by juniors and seniors. The school district honored him as Teacher of the Year. One day while Ras was out of the room, we asked his students why they thought he received these honors. Their answers were basically threefold: "He respects us," "He listens to us," and "He enjoys his job."

"What does enjoying the job have to do with anything?" we asked. One of the students explained, "Many teachers come to work with an attitude problem. They hate us. They hate their jobs. They seem to hate life. They take it out on us. Ras is always up. He seems to enjoy us, his job, life in general—and us."

Ras has a unique way of making sure the message of caring (connection) gets through. He keeps a teddy bear in his classroom. He introduces the bear to his students and says, "This is our care bear. If any of you feel discouraged or a little down, come get the bear. He'll make you feel better." At first the students think Ras is bonkers. After all, they are high school juniors and seniors, young adults. But they soon catch the spirit. Every day several students, including the big football players, go to Ras's desk and say, "I need the bear."

The bear became so popular that Ras had to provide more bears to keep up with the demand. Sometimes the kids carry them around all day, but they always bring them back. Sometimes, when Ras sees a student who looks a little down, he tosses a bear to the student. This is his symbolic way of saying, "I care. I don't have time to spend with you personally right now, but I care."

TAKE A FIELD TRIP

Middle school teacher Brenda Rollins wrote on her Facebook page, "Home and showered after taking 73 middle school students on a bicycle field trip. The skunks running through the campsite all night and the raccoon in the tent were amusing, but now exhausted." Later, in answer to a question about whether the kids had a good time, she wrote, "They all had a good time; most had no idea they could ride 7 miles, or go to the park, or get anywhere on a bike."

Brenda, along with two other teachers, two parents, and ten bike enthusiasts, made this a positive experience for new students. Not only was it fun, it was a way for the kids to bond with each other and the teachers to get to know the kids better outside the classroom and make a connection with them. Brenda's school, the Santa Rosa Charter School, a Positive Discipline school, encourages field trips throughout the year, including a trip to Ashland, Oregon, to attend the Shakespeare Festival. These trips are a time for kids, teachers, and parents to celebrate the joy of learning and being together and having educational adventures.

APPRECIATE UNIQUENESS

One teacher made a set of baseball cards for his third-grade class. Each card featured a student's picture and nickname. The nicknames expressed the unique interest of each child. For example, one card said, "Cat-Lover Colleen," and another, "Home-Run Sean." Although it takes time and skill to make a set of baseball cards, it can be fun to let the kids come up with nicknames together, as long as the activity remains respectful.

Another way of expressing each student's uniqueness is to have them create their own T-shirts. You might also do this activity with other teachers during a faculty meeting.

ACTIVITY: CREATE YOUR OWN T-SHIRT

OBJECTIVE

To help students and teachers become aware of their uniqueness and the uniqueness of others

MATERIALS

Masking tape

Pieces of paper in the shape of T-shirts (one for each student)

Instructions written on a flip chart or the board

1. Write your name at the top of the shirt.

2. In the middle of the shirt, write one word that describes you.

3. All over the shirt, write words that describe some of your characteristics and special interests.

4. Across the bottom of the shirt, write one thing about you that most people probably don't know.

DIRECTIONS

1. Allow about ten minutes for students to create their T-shirts.

2. Ask students to tape their T-shirts onto their clothes.

3. Have students form groups of three to five and share their T-shirts with their group.

4. Have students walk around the room to look for others who have similar characteristics and interests.

5. Then have students find a person who does not have a similar characteristic or interest and to ask each other questions about what they see on the other's shirt.

6. At the end of the activity, process with the class about what they learned. Ask such questions as:

What did you learn from this activity?
How many of you found someone who had an interest that you would like to know more about?
How many of you found people with similar interests and characteristics?
How many of you realize you have a talent that could be used to help others?
How many of you found others who have strengths that could be helpful to you?

USE YOUR SENSE OF HUMOR
TO CREATE A CONNECTION

Sometimes teachers forget to see the humor in situations with students. Contrary to what some beginning teachers are told, it's okay not to be serious all the time. Mrs. Turner plays a game called Let's Make a Deal with her class, and the kids love it. She says, "Okay kids, it's time for Let's Make a Deal. I like to start on time, and you like to leave on time. I'll save up the time I have to wait to get started, and you can make it up after school. Deal?" The kids groan and then settle down.

Some teachers use sarcasm in the guise of humor to put students down. Others may go for a laugh at a student's expense. This is not respectful. The feeling behind what you do is as important as what you do.

Mr. Barkley has a droll sense of humor that kids love. They know he cares about them and about whether they succeed in school. They sense the feeling behind what he does, and his caring comes through.

One day Mr. Barkley was dealing with a daydreaming student. He put his hand lightly on the boy's shoulder and said, "Picture this. You're eighteen years old. You get up and turn on MTV. You know everyone on the videos and all the words to the songs. But will anyone give you a job? No way! And why not? Because you spent all your time in my class staring into space." The student looked up, grinned, and opened his book.

Later in the period Jennifer was passing notes to a friend and paying no attention to a play Mr. Barkley was reading to the class. In a smooth but slightly louder voice, Mr. Barkley read, "To be or not to be, that is the question Jennifer asks herself each day." She looked up and said, "Huh? Were you calling on me?" Mr. Barkley said, "Did anyone hear me call on Jennifer? I don't think so." Jennifer paid attention for the rest of class. If there is sincere caring for the kids, they will get the message.

CREATE CONNECTION BY RESPECTING STUDENTS' OUTSIDE INTERESTS

It's easy to forget that students have interests in life other than school. Their social life is extremely important to them, and often they are coping with issues of rejection or popularity. They may be dealing with the upset of not being chosen for teams or never being the first or the best. By the time kids reach junior high and high school, they may have job issues, car issues, dating issues, sex issues, and drug issues.

Many kids operate according to a different clock than adults do. They like to stay up late and then have difficulty getting up in the morning. Yet they have to conform to an early start at school.

We saw this note pasted on a door of a high school classroom in Charlotte, North Carolina: "Tardies, please come into the room quietly, find a seat, look for your directions on the board. Learning begins as soon as the tardy bell rings." Instead of humiliating or punishing latecomers, this teacher respectfully allows students to experience the consequences and do what they need to do to catch up. Students can come in and start working right away instead of going to the office, getting papers, feeling like they're in trouble, and disturbing the class.

Another teacher tells his students, "I won't take roll until five minutes after the tardy bell. I know some of you have jobs and have a difficult time handling all the demands of being a teenager. It would be better if you could sleep in until ten, go to school until five, and have the rest of the evening for family time, jobs, and a social life." The kids cheer. They do their best not to take advantage. They respect this teacher because they feel respected. He knows how to make sure the message of caring gets through.

Respect invites respect. Disrespect invites disrespect. When a teacher's students are acting disrespectfully, that teacher might take a look at his or her own behavior.

IMPROVEMENT, NOT PERFECTION

Students know that teachers care when they encourage improvement, rather than perfection. Classrooms may never be perfect, but every failure can provide an opportunity for coming up with solutions. Even if you feel discouraged or take steps backward while slowly moving forward, continue asking, "What can we do to solve this problem?" Not only does this question show that you care, it encourages kids to care about each other.

In one school, a girl was killed in a car accident. The crisis team decided to use Class Meetings to help students deal with their grief and fears. At these meetings, students celebrated how this little girl had touched them—each student had a chance to express an appreciation for her. Then the teachers asked, "What are your concerns now?" Some students said they were afraid to go home. Many had never dealt with death before and didn't know what to do.

Students brainstormed and found several suggestions. One was to set up a phone tree so they could call each other, even in the middle of the night. The students came up with a list of people they could talk to during the day. Many students had different people they felt they could talk to during school hours: janitors, librarians, a lunchroom supervisor, counselors, teachers, the principal, and one another. They were able to get passes to go talk to someone whenever they felt the need. The students also decided to make pictures of the girl on a ribbon pin, which

POSITIVE DISCIPLINE IN ACTION

Over and over and over again I am grateful to the Santa Rosa Charter School. They have given my children not only a healthy love of learning, but a solid sense of how to behave like a decent human being whether you agree with someone or not. The most beautiful thing of all is that even my kids (the youngest now 13 and in her last year at the school) get that.... The Santa Rosa Charter School is part of the Santa Rosa Education Cooperative, an umbrella organization for the fee-based preschool and public charter school K–8. The preschool was the foundation school for the charter. Without the preschool and the founders wanting their children to continue in a PD and cooperative environment, there would be no charter. At Santa Rosa Education Cooperative, all the classes use Class Meetings and the kids learn and use the Eight Skills for Class Meetings.

Sabrina Howell, mother of three students
at the Santa Rosa Charter School, a
Positive Discipline school in Santa Rosa, California

they wore for a week in her memory. They bought a tree, which they planted and nurtured throughout the year to remember her. The students became role models for adult school members on their many ways to deal with grief.

A teacher who is willing to teach students connection skills often finds that his or her job becomes easier and more fun. Helping students experience caring, belonging, and significance is the most powerful thing a teacher can do—motivating them to fulfill their highest potential, academically and otherwise.

POSITIVE DISCIPLINE IN ACTION

When I began my first year of teaching fifteen years ago, I knew I needed to implement a behavior management system, but I didn't know how to choose one or put it into practice. What I had seen in other classrooms, and read about in books, were authoritarian systems involving students moving clips, flipping color-coded cards, and having their names written on the board. I went ahead and tried one of those systems, but my only litmus test for whether it was working was if the students were silent and chose to follow my every direction at a moment's notice. This certainly was not the case, so I decided that the system wasn't working, and that I needed to try another . . . and another . . . and another! That sure was a rough year!

I spent much of that year feeling frustrated, helpless, and powerless. I often raised my voice, clenched my jaw, and quite honestly, cried. At the end of the year, I decided that I would commit to a second year of teaching but vowed not to have a repeat performance of the first. I knew so much about what I *didn't* want to do again. I knew that I wanted to help each of my students achieve as much academic success as possible, but what was more important to me was to try and really see them for who they were and connect with them on a personal level. It became abundantly clear that without that personal connection, no real academic success was going to be possible.

During the next ten years, much of what I did and felt while teaching fits closely with Positive Discipline. It wasn't until 2007, though, that I came upon the books *Positive Discipline in the Classroom* and *Positive Discipline: A Teacher's A-Z Guide*. I know it sounds silly, but as I read the books, I couldn't help but think I was hearing angels sing! Everything I read sounded and felt so right to me. I was amazed because so much of what I saw there on the pages was what I'd been feeling but hadn't been able to verbalize.

In the summer of 2008, I went to a two-day Positive Discipline in the Classroom workshop. I loved every minute of it. I was so excited to get back to school to use my new tools! I began implementing Positive Discipline with my students, and I informally shared with their parents what I had learned from the books and the workshop. I began holding Class Meetings. The process did not always go smoothly, but my students and their ideas for solving problems amazed me. On the last day of school, my students and I looked at the stack of agenda sheets we'd used throughout the year. It was at least two inches high! My students were so proud that they'd been able to work together to solve so many problems. (I was proud, too!)

I have continued to use Positive Discipline in my classroom, but this past year I felt I needed to drop Class Meetings. With the expanding number of activities and lessons required by the administration, I just didn't think I could make the time for them. As I reflect on the frustrating year we had, though, I see that many, if not all, of the behavior and classroom issues that drove me crazy could have been addressed during Class Meetings. Class Meetings were exactly what my students and I needed. Dropping them was a big mistake. How helpful it is, though, that thanks to Positive Discipline, I know that mistakes are wonderful opportunities to learn!

Anonymous

6

RESPECTFUL
COMMUNICATION SKILLS

All opinions are correct from the point of view of the observer.

RUDOLF DREIKURS

Improving our communication skills is an ongoing process. This chapter is about assessing your skills and adding tools where needed. In Chapter 7, we'll share activities you can do with your students to help them communicate better in the classroom.

This Thermometer Activity will demonstrate the difference between poor communication skills and effective ones. Try it with a friend to see what you learn.

Ask your friend to role-play a student who will pretend there is a thermometer on the floor between you. When you use words that are discouraging, he or she is to move away from you (to the cold end of the thermometer) and when you use words that feel encouraging, he or she is to move closer to you (to the warm end of the thermometer). Let the "student" know that he or she need not respond with words—just movement indicating discouragement (moving back to the cold end) and encouragement (moving forward to the warm end).

Start by using any of the following communication blocks. We know you wouldn't really talk to kids this way, but we've made the examples extreme to help speed up the learning process. You can use an accusing voice as you say the following, one sentence at a time.

Communication Blocks

This is your fault.

How many times do I have to go over this with you? Do you have cotton in your ears?

The other students have been complaining about your behavior, and I believe them.

When are you ever going to shape up?

I'm not interested in how you feel. Stop crying and acting like a baby!

What did you do? Don't tell me you didn't do anything!

You better figure out how to do what you're told, or you might get an F in this class.

By now, the "student" has probably moved to the cold end of the thermometer. Ask what he or she was learning during this phase of the activity.

Now tell the "student" you would like to try again. Again, he or she should move to the cold or warm end of the thermometer based on what you say. The following are sentences designed to improve communication, though it might take a while to win back the "student's" trust.

Communication Improvers

I can see that you're feeling very upset right now. I understand. It is upsetting.

The yard duty supervisor told me you weren't being cooperative today. I'm interested in hearing your version of what happened?

If you need any help with this problem, let me know. I may have some ideas.

Why don't you put this on the agenda for the Class Meeting so you can tell the other students your side of the story?

Can you think of some ways to avoid this problem in the future?

Thanks for taking the time to talk with me about this.

Once again, ask the "student" to share what he or she was learning. Share with that person what you were thinking, feeling, and deciding in both versions. What did you learn from this activity about how communication deteriorates in the classroom and what you can do to improve it?

CHANGING FROM COMMUNICATION THAT BLOCKS CONNECTION TO COMMUNICATION THAT PROMOTES CONNECTION

Stephen Glenn describes five Barriers and Builders for Communication.* Often, we use barriers while thinking we are improving communication.

---

* On Barriers and Builders, see H. Stephen Glenn and Jane Nelsen, *Raising Self-Reliant Children in a Self-Indulgent World* (New York: Three Rivers Press, 2002), which devotes a chapter to the subject. It is also taught in the Developing Capable People course. Call 1-800-456-7770 for more information.

1. BARRIER ASSUMING VERSUS CHECKING

It is easy to assume that you know what students think and feel without asking them. You may assume what they can or can't do and how they should or shouldn't respond. We call this mind reading, and we've yet to find an adult whom we would consider a certified mind reader. If you treat someone according to your assumptions, not only might you miss out on who they really are, but you could also damage the relationship by inadvertently hurting their feelings.

Instead of assuming, you can build communication by checking—asking Curiosity Questions. Positive Discipline methods encourage teachers to discover what students actually think and feel. When you check instead of assume, you discover what students are really thinking and feeling about problems and issues that affect them.

One special education teacher trained in behavior modification assumed that her students were incapable of participating in Class Meetings; she believed it was her job simply to control their behavior. She was encouraged to test her assumption by trying a Class Meeting. Even though the children couldn't write their names, each had a special mark they could stamp on the agenda to signify they wanted help with a problem. The teacher discovered that the children were more capable than she had assumed. They quickly learned to express their needs at the Class Meeting and engaged in problem solving far beyond the teacher's assumptions.

Another teacher assumed that a group of girls were having trouble playing together because there were three of them. This teacher was convinced that three girls couldn't play together without one of them being ostracized. When she checked with the girls about what was going on, they said, "Teacher, we like to play together. We just can't figure out how to divide things three ways when we only have two balls." Given that the girls were in kindergarten, the teacher asked if they would like some suggestions on how to share two balls three ways. They were excited to hear her ideas. They especially liked the idea of using one ball at a time and throwing it to each other in turn. When the teacher suggested they take turns watching the other two play, they laughed. The teacher said, "How about the girl with the curliest hair watch first? Then the girl with the straightest hair watch second, and finally, the girl with the shortest hair watch third." The girls told the teacher, "Thanks. We can figure it out." And they did, and their solution was easier than the teacher's suggestions. They used Roshambo (rock-paper-scissors) as their system for missing a turn.

2. RESCUING AND EXPLAINING VERSUS EXPLORING

Rescuing and explaining are blocks to communication. You may think you are being caring or helpful when you do things for students instead of allowing them to learn from their own experiences. Likewise, you may think you're being helpful by explaining things to students instead of letting them discover the explanation for themselves. You might find it interesting to tally the number of times you try to rescue students while giving them a lecture, explaining what happened, what caused it to happen, how they should feel about it, and what they should do. For example, a teacher might take a child by the hand and find her coat for her while delivering a lecture on responsibility. You might also find it interesting to observe the blank look on a student's face to see if, by any chance, he or she is as interested in the lecture as you are. Rudolf Dreikurs suggested it is best never to do for a child what the child can do for him- or herself.

Exploring is the communication builder. Again, use curiosity to promote connection and improved communication. The Asking Versus Telling Activity in Chapter 2 is a great activity to help you become more curious. A very simple way to explore is to ask, "Tell me more." You can follow that up with "And then? And then?" Kids don't need much encouragement to tell you what they think and how they feel. They do need to know that you are genuinely interested in their point of view. As long as you listen without judging, interrupting, or correcting, they'll tell you a lot.

Class meetings are opportunities for students to explore what happened, what caused it to happen, how behavior affects others, how they feel about it, and what they can do to solve the problem. If you provide the opportunity to use their own wisdom, students will often come to the same conclusions that they seem to ignore when given to them through adult lectures. This kind of exploration helps students develop an internal, rather than an external, locus of control.

3. DIRECTING VERSUS INVITING AND ENCOURAGING

Issuing too many directives reinforces dependence, eliminates initiative and cooperation, and encourages passive-aggressive behavior (grudgingly doing the minimum amount of work and leaving as much undone as possible in order to "bug" the teacher). If you aren't sure whether you use this barrier to communication, it's easy to find out by doing a reality check. If you notice that you have to repeat yourself constantly and complain that students aren't listening, you may be guilty of giving too many directives. If that's the case, you could work on the communication builder of inviting and encouraging.

Involve students in the planning and problem-solving activities that help them become self-directed: "The bell will ring soon. I would appreciate anything you could do to help me get the room straightened up for the next class." Directing invites passive or active resistance and/or rebellion. Inviting encourages cooperation.

4. EXPECTING VERSUS CELEBRATING

It is important for teachers to have high expectations for young people and to believe in their potential. However, if that potential becomes the standard, and you judge students negatively for falling short, you discourage them. For example, "I was expecting more maturity from you. I thought you were more responsible than that. I expected you to be the kind of student your brother was."

Instead of expecting, look for opportunities to celebrate accomplishment and uniqueness. Class Meetings allow teachers and students to acknowledge one another through compliments and problem solving. With practice, you'll find that this skill spills over from Class Meetings to use throughout the day. When you quickly celebrate any movement in the direction of a student's potential or maturity, you encourage. When you demand too much too soon, you discourage.

Suppose a student who has never risked asking a question suddenly asks a question, but it's unrelated to the topic being discussed. You could affirm that student for asking a question instead of criticizing him or her for not paying attention, then ask if he or she has anything to say about the topic being discussed. Students who cheat can be affirmed for their desire to get a better grade, then be invited to explore other ways to accomplish that goal.

5. "ADULTISMS" VERSUS RESPECTING

"Adultisms" occur when teachers forget that children are not mature adults and expect them to think and act like adults. Examples: "How come you never _____?" "Why can't you ever _____?" "Surely you realize _____?" "How many times do I have to tell you?" "I can't believe you would do such a thing! You are such a disappointment." Almost anything that begins with the words *should* or *ought* or with an angry tone of voice is an adultism. Adultisms produce guilt and shame rather than support and encouragement. The message is *Since you don't see what I see, you are at fault.*

When you practice respect, you acknowledge that you and your students have different points of view. Respect creates a climate of acceptance that encourages growth and effective communication. Instead of judging people for what they don't see, encourage students to seek understanding of themselves and others. Instead of saying, "You knew what I wanted on this project!" say, "What is your understanding of the requirements for this project?" or "What were you thinking of when you presented your project this way?" If you aren't interested in hearing the answer, don't ask the question.

Students often don't have the same priorities as adults. Doing well in math and science or in school in general may not even be in students' top-hundred list of priorities. This does not mean that they should not be required to study math and science. It does mean that teachers must show respect and understanding that students have other priorities, such as friends (or not having any), sports (or not being chosen for the team), cars ("Will I ever be able to afford one?"), sleeping in ("Doesn't my teacher know I'm on a different time clock?"), or good or bad family relationships. The list goes on and on.

Class meetings are opportunities for students to explore and resolve many of the issues that are troubling them. You can then use some student issues and priorities to help them explore the relevance of learning. Through these methods, you can invite students to cooperate instead of to resist and rebel.

• • •

The communication barriers create frustration and discouragement for teachers and students alike. Switching to the Five Builders for Communication empowers both. When teachers think of students as people, they find it easier to empower students by checking, exploring, inviting and encouraging, celebrating, and respecting. A teacher tells the following story:

> *I realized that I was using barriers with my students. I assumed they needed me to step in and take care of things, explain things, direct them where to go and what to do, and to point out where they fell short of my expectations for the day by "shoulding" on them. Then I ended up lecturing, using expressions such as "How many times must I tell you?" or "You know better than that!" I felt exhausted, and the students weren't progressing.*
>
> *I switched to builders. I checked the students' understanding of a problem, explored their perceptions of how to work with it, invited their assistance in finding a solution, celebrated any movement in the desired direction rather than pointing out where they fell short of my expectations, and showed respect for them by honoring their thoughts and feelings. The classroom atmosphere improved; so did my disposition and the kids' progress.*

No one technique is better than another, but it's important to remember that communication isn't simply about talking. A lot of listening, respect, curiosity, and empowerment goes on during good communication. If you'd like to work on other communication skills, choose one of the following to practice.

FOUR EMPOWERING COMMUNICATION TECHNIQUES

1. SAY IT, MEAN IT

Students can tell when you mean what you say and when you're just making noise. How does that happen? Kids are very scientific. They hear your actions more than they hear your words. If you spend a lot of time talking, directing, demanding, and telling, but you don't follow through with action, your words go in one ear and out the other. They become "teacher deaf."

On the other hand, if you say something once and follow through with action, students know you mean business. They pay attention. The tricky part is that you have to think carefully before you say something to make sure it's something you can follow through on with action.

For example, Teacher Jones says, "When you're lined up quietly, we'll head to the playground." She doesn't say another word; instead, she waits quietly until the students are in a quiet line, then opens the classroom door and proceeds to the playground.

Teacher Singer says, "Late papers get a zero." Susie turns in a late paper, and it is returned to her with a zero. She complains, whines, and begs Teacher Singer to change his mind. Teacher Singer smiles and says, "Good try, Susie," then moves on to something else.

Two students come to Teacher Smith, blaming each other for a problem. Teacher Smith says, "I'm not interested in finding out who is at fault. Instead, we can work on solving problems together. She adds the issue to the Class Meeting agenda, saying, "I'm sure we'll sort this out at our next Class Meeting."

2. LESS IS MORE

If you notice that your students aren't paying attention and that things seem to be getting more and more out of control, work on reducing the number of words you say. Try saying things using one word or a short sentence of ten words or less.

Think about what your students hear when you say, "Recess." "Quiet." "Time." "Circle." (All one word.) Or "Pencils down and

POSITIVE DISCIPLINE IN ACTION

I first came in contact with the Positive Discipline program about twenty years ago when I started using it in my classroom. Wow—what a difference it made in helping to create a wonderful environment for young children! Everything I read in the book made perfect sense. Parents approached me about changes they noticed in their children at home. Conversations then followed about Class Meetings and family meetings. Since I was a parent as well, I began to use Positive Discipline techniques at home with my own kids and was really impressed at how well they worked in helping to develop mutual respect.

Christine Hamilton, Eugene, Oregon

papers to the front, please" (eight words). "Raise hands if you're ready for a story" (eight words). "Look for solutions on the Wheel of Choice" (eight words). "Class meeting time" (three words). "Messy room. Time to clean up papers on the floor" (ten words).

You'll be surprised at how attentive your students get when you practice this simple skill. Make sure you say your word or short sentence once, and then wait quietly for the students to process it and start moving.

3. HEAD, HEART, GUT

Most of the time we speak from our heads. In the classroom, it's okay to *speak from our hearts and guts*, using feeling words. Here's how the same information sounds when coming from the head, the heart, and the gut. As you read the examples, think about your response to each.

HEAD   "There's too much pushing and hitting and hurting going on at the playground when you're playing Four Square. I think it may be time to ban that game. We can't have that kind of behavior on the playground."

HEART   "I saw someone get hit with a ball during Four Square and end up with a black and blue mark. That upset me. I'm worried that we won't be able to play that game if we can't figure out how to play it safely and respectfully."

GUT   "I'm angry that some of you use Four Square as a way of hurting others. I'm banning that game until you guys can convince me you can try again playing respectfully and safely. Let me know when you have come up with a plan."

Close your eyes, pretend you are a student, and listen while someone reads aloud each of the above statements from the head, heart, and gut. Which one would have the greatest impact on you? One person shared that the Head statement sounded like, "blah, blah, blah." The Heart statement sounded like, "Teacher is upset again. What else is new." But the Gut statement really got her attention. Pretending she was a child, she felt concerned that the teacher was angry and wanted to come up with a plan to make sure they could keep playing.

Many people who are drawn to Positive Discipline don't have trouble with fulfilling the "kind" part of "be kind and firm at the same time," but they have trouble with the "firm" part. Sharing from your gut is one of the best ways to express the "firm" part, and it is especially effective when you add a respectful call for action.

POSITIVE DISCIPLINE IN ACTION

We look at our program as a triangle: student-parent-guide (teacher). We have very clear expectations of what we expect from each side of the triangle, and we honor what each person brings to the process. One of the things that we have found very helpful is to strongly encourage all new parents who join the school community to take a Positive Discipline parenting class. We try to be clear that we're not attempting to "change their parenting," and we try to avoid implying that they aren't parenting "right." We explain to them that by taking the class, they will be able to speak the same language that the guides and administration do when discussing discipline and classroom management, which will allow us to work together better as a team. That often opens them to taking the classes, and most of them take Positive Discipline back into their homes.

Molly Henry, director of a Montessori school

4. TENNIS MATCH

Think about what it's like to play or watch a great tennis match. The long rallies where the ball is going back and forth, back and forth, are exciting. But how much fun would it be if someone served the ball and no one could ever return it? You'd probably lose interest pretty quickly.

That's what happens in a one-sided conversation. A great conversations is like a tennis match, where the dialogue goes back and forth, back and forth, with both people taking turns and sharing thoughts and feelings. Sometimes a two-way conversation may not be appropriate in a classroom, but at other times it's imperative.

Imagine asking one of your students to come talk with you after school about a problem with his or her studies. That's the time for the tennis match conversation. Or how about on a field trip when you have an opportunity to hang out with students? In Class Meetings students learn how to take turns while being engaged in listening to what others have to say.

You can use experiential activities to teach communication skills to your students. Most students have fun learning from the following three activities.

ACTIVITY: LISTENING SKILLS 1

OBJECTIVE
To teach effective listening skills

COMMENT
It is often easier to talk than to be a good listener. Developing good listening skills requires practice.

DIRECTIONS
1. Have all your students work in pairs. Pick a topic like "my favorite food for dinner" or "what I like about school" or "what I don't like about school." Tell your students to talk about that topic all at the same time.

2. Signal for them to stop, then ask how many of them felt that they were heard. A lively discussion may result as students express what they were feeling, learning, or deciding.

3. Ask the students what they could do to solve the problem of all talking at once. What do they need to do to be good listeners?

4. Record all of their ideas on poster paper labeled "Good Listening Skills." It might look like this (but it is important that your students create their own):

- Use eye contact. (Don't let your eyes wander.)
- Don't interrupt.
- Nod once in a while to indicate that you are listening.
- Be interested and curious about what the other person has to say.
- Give the speaker your full attention.

5. Hang the poster in the room. Later, if students do not use good listening skills, refer to the poster to find something they could do to improve.

ACTIVITY: LISTENING SKILLS 2

DIRECTIONS

1. Have students work in pairs. First, one student tells the other about a favorite TV show, while the other refuses to make eye contact. Second, the listening partner actually gets up and walks away while the other is still talking.

2. Ask the students to share their thoughts, feelings, and decisions about their experience. Ask those who were acting "rudely," even though they were just role-playing, to apologize for not being good listeners and to try again. This is good practice for students to learn that it is okay to make a mistake, correct it, and try again. It will also help the person who felt slighted be more ready to cooperate with the next part of the activity.

3. First, the talking student in each pair once more tells his or her partner about a favorite TV show. This time, at your instruction, the partner listens carefully and uses eye contact and body language that shows interest, such as leaning closer.

4. Process again about both students' thoughts, feelings, and decisions based on this experience.

COMMENT

Even though it is only a role-play, the disheartening part of this activity can leave students with feelings of discouragement.

As students express what they learn from these activities, you will find that everyone is getting the message about poor listening skills. Discuss with students how the quality of listening skills relates to the success of Class Meetings—and to success in life.

ACTIVITY: "I" STATEMENTS

OBJECTIVE

Communication is improved when you talk about what is happening inside of you instead of analyzing others. This activity helps you name your feelings and share them openly with others, inviting better communication all around.

DIRECTIONS

1. Part of good communication is to use "I" statements. Have students practice "I" statements by thinking of a time when they were very happy.

2. Have students fill in the blanks to the following sentence: "I felt happy when _____, and I wish _____."

3. Then have students think of a time when they were angry and fill in the blanks to the following sentence: "I felt angry when _____, and I wish _____."

COMMENT

Feelings can usually be expressed in one word. You may want students to develop a list of feelings, such as *happy, angry, embarrassed, afraid, sad, excited,* and so on, or refer to the Feeling Faces chart for more practice.

Once students learn the skill of using "I" statements, they will have a reference point for when communication breaks down. For instance, if you think a student is communicating in a blaming or judgmental way, you might ask him or her, "Would you be willing to try that again using an 'I' statement, or would you like help from the class?" If the student wants help, let him or her choose a suggestion from someone whose hand is raised.

Positive Discipline
Feeling Faces

7

FOCUSING ON SOLUTIONS

There are no ills created by democracy that can't be cured by more democracy.

RUDOLF DREIKURS

C an you imagine what your classroom would be like if all your students were focusing on solutions? Actually, can you imagine what the world would be like if everyone focused on solutions? We would have global peace. But many students are so used to punishment that they have accepted this as the way things should be. The following activity will help them think more deeply and come to some different conclusions.

DO YOU HAVE TO FEEL WORSE TO DO BETTER?

Ask a volunteer to make the following poster to help the class remember that encouragement is more effective than punishment:

WHERE DID WE EVER GET THE CRAZY IDEA
THAT TO MAKE PEOPLE DO BETTER, WE FIRST HAVE
TO MAKE THEM FEEL WORSE?
PEOPLE DO BETTER WHEN THEY FEEL BETTER.

Ask your students to think of a time when someone tried to motivate them to do better by making them feel worse. Pass out sheets of paper with the following three headings: MY PUNISHMENT, WHAT I DECIDED ABOUT MYSELF AND/OR OTHERS, AND WHAT I DECIDED TO DO.

Then ask the students to list as many things as they can think of under the MY PUNISHMENT heading. Possibilities include grounding, spanking, scolding, and taking away privileges—ask them to add any of these punishments that fit for them. Ask them to remember exactly what happened, as though they were reliving the event, and to recall how they felt.

Ask them to fill in the columns under WHAT I DECIDED ABOUT MYSELF AND/OR OTHERS AND WHAT I DECIDED TO DO.

MY PUNISHMENT	WHAT I DECIDED ABOUT MYSELF AND/OR OTHERS	WHAT I DECIDED TO DO
Stay after class	The teacher is stupid.	Stay after and pretend to work.
Call my parents	I'm in trouble. I need to figure out how to get out of it.	Tell my parents the teacher lied.
Write sentences	This is boring and stupid. I better not get caught again.	Write the sentences and then do what I want.
Put name on board	I don't care.	Experience the punishment but don't change.
Got a red card	I am bad.	Give up because I'm a bad person.

Share the following example with your students. Ask, "How many of you think that the student in the chart is deciding to be more responsible and cooperative in the future? What other things do you think this student might be deciding to do in the future?"

Invite your students to share how they answered the same questions. Then ask what they learned from this activity. Ask if they would be willing to learn more respectful ways to help each other improve their behavior—ways that don't include any punishment. Probably not many students would resist this invitation. Tell your students that they can learn how to brainstorm for solutions that are better than punishment—and even better than consequences (which are often poorly disguised punishment).

Some classes have adopted the slogans (and made posters) that say "We are not looking for blame, we are looking for solutions" and "What is the challenge? What is the solution?" As you offer more and more ways for students to focus on solutions, excitement will grow for these encouraging processes. Here are six more ways to focus on solutions:

THREE R'S AND AN H FOR SOLUTIONS

Just as students need training and practice to learn academic skills, they need training and practice to learn problem-solving skills. The following activity will help.

1. Inform students that, in the future, their job will be to find solutions to solve problems that do not include punishment.
2. Have the class imagine that one girl has written on the desk of another. On the board, list the following five suggestions for solving that problem:
   - Have the girl sit on the floor for a week.
   - Have the girl clean all the desks in the room.

- Make the girl clean the other girl's desk while everyone watches.
- Have the girl apologize.
- Ask the girl if she would like to clean the other girl's desk now or before she leaves for the day.

3. Now tell the students about the Three R's and an H for Solutions:
   - Related
   - Respectful
   - Reasonable
   - Helpful

4. Share the following definitions with your students:
   - **Related:** The solution should be directly related to the behavior. For example, suppose some students didn't do their homework. Sending them to the office is not related to homework. A solution that is related to the behavior would be for them to make up the homework or to not get points for that assignment.
   - **Respectful:** Whatever the solution is, teachers and students should maintain a respectful attitude in their manner and tone of voice. The teachers also should follow up on the solution with dignity and respect. "Would you like to make up the homework assignment during lunch recess or right after school?" It also means that students know in advance what their choices will be if they make a mistake. When kids know in advance, it is their choice. When they don't, it's arbitrary and up to the teacher, leaving the student at the mercy of the teacher.
   - **Reasonable:** The solution should be reasonable—don't add punishment. For example, don't say something like "Now you'll have to do twice as much" or "Now I'll have to send a note home to your parents and suggest they take away privileges at home, too."
   - **Helpful:** The solution should help the student do better. It should help solve the problem.

5. Go over the list of suggestions about the girl who wrote on the other girl's desk. For each suggestion, ask, by a show of hands, "How many think this suggestion is related, respectful, reasonable, and helpful?" Cross out the suggestions that don't fit the Three R's and an H for Solutions criteria. Point out that when a solution meets all four criteria, it will probably be a good alternative to punishment.

Once students have brainstormed solutions to a problem, it is extremely important to let the individual student choose the solution he or she thinks will be most helpful. This encourages accountability to blossom in a safe environment.

THE FOUR PROBLEM-SOLVING STEPS

These four steps provide a process and another guide that helps students stay on track while finding a solution to problems. Begin by sharing the Four Problem-Solving Steps with your students.

1. Ignore the problem. (It takes more courage to walk way than to stay and confront, fight, or argue.)
   - Do something else. (Find another game or activity.)
   - Leave long enough for a cooling-off period, and then follow-up with the next steps.

2. Talk it over respectfully.
   - Tell the other person how you feel. Let him or her know you don't like what's happening.
   - Listen to what the other person says about how he or she feels and what he or she doesn't like.
   - Share what you think you did to contribute to the problem.
   - Tell the other person what you are willing to do differently.

3. Agree on a solution. For example:
   - Work out a plan for sharing or taking turns.
   - Figure out how to make amends.
   - Figure out how to repair damage.
4. If you can't work it out together, ask for help.
   - Put it on the Class Meeting agenda.
   - Talk it over with a parent, teacher, or friend.

Have your students role-play the following hypothetical situations. Have them solve each of the situations four different ways (one for each of the steps).

- Fighting over whose turn it is to use the tetherball
- Shoving in line
- Calling people names
- Fighting over whose turn it is to sit by the window in the bus or car

After you teach the Four Problem-Solving Steps, ask for volunteers to make a poster of the steps. Once it is made, place it in an area where your students can refer to it. Some teachers have the steps on wallet-size laminated cards that their students can carry with them and use as needed. One school painted the Four Problem-Solving Steps on a playground problem-solving bench.

Mrs. Underwood allows her students to leave the room at any time to use the Problem-Solving Steps. Quite often she will watch two children leave the room and then see them sitting by the fence talking. A few minutes later they come back to the classroom and go about their business.

THE TOOL CARD BASKET

Some teachers become uncomfortable when we advocate focusing on solutions instead of punishments and rewards. They wonder, *What else is there?*

As you have already discovered, this book is filled with alternatives. Another alternative that focuses on solutions is to the deck of Positive Discipline Tool Cards. Here are some examples:

These Tool Cards were designed for parents and children to use in homes, but most of them are equally effective in the classroom. They can be purchased at www.positivediscipline.com.

You might want to choose the cards from the deck that represent solutions that could work in your classroom and put them in a basket somewhere in the room. When students have a problem, one of their choices is to go to the basket and randomly choose a card to see if that solution would work. They can pull out as many as three cards and choose the one they think would work the best.

To make sure students understand all the solutions on the cards, once a week ask a student to pick a card and bring it to the circle for discussion. Ask the whole group to share their understanding of what the card means. If the kids need clarification, explain and give examples for the students to role-play. The more problem-solving skills kids have, the less time you will need to devote to solving problems for them.

THE WHEEL OF CHOICE

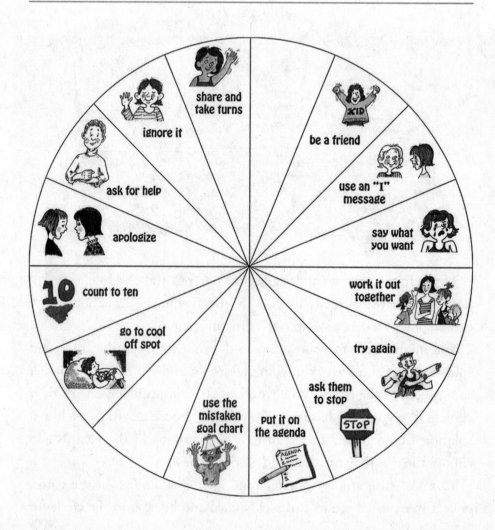

The Wheel of Choice, see picture on previous page, is another way to empower children to solve their own problems instead of putting pressure on the teacher to be the sole problem solver. Each of the slices on the Wheel of Choice refers to a problem-solving skill that children can learn and then use. In the process, they have alternatives to disrespectful methods. The skills in the Wheel of Choice give a grounding in respect for others, cooperation, and confidence in their capabilities.

Since *Positive Discipline in the Classroom* was first published, many teachers have loved using the Wheel of Choice in their classrooms—without lesson plans. After all, don't all students know how to do something as simple as count to ten to calm down, or to share and take turns? At some level they do, and the Wheel of Choice has been effective. However, the teachers who helped create fourteen lesson plans 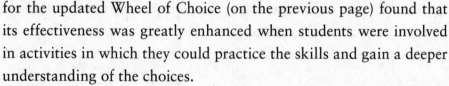 for the updated Wheel of Choice (on the previous page) found that its effectiveness was greatly enhanced when students were involved in activities in which they could practice the skills and gain a deeper understanding of the choices.

After the students practice the skills, they color in the appropriate slice to create their personal Wheel of Choice. All fourteen lesson plans are available at www.positivediscipline.com. The lesson on "Apologize" follows.

ACTIVITY: APOLOGIZE

OBJECTIVE
To teach kids how to offer a sincere apology

MATERIAL
Crayons or marking pens for coloring individual Wheels of Choice

COMMENT
Sometimes when you make a mistake, you have to make amends where possible, and at least apologize when not possible. Apologies create a connection so that people are ready to work on solutions.

DIRECTIONS
1. Teach that making mistakes is not as important as what people do about them. Anyone can make mistakes, but it takes a secure person to say, "I'm sorry," and to make amends if possible.

2. Ask your kids to think of a time when their feelings were hurt by another person who gave them an insincere apology, saying "I'm sorry" when they didn't mean it.

3. In classrooms, have your students get in pairs and give each other fake apologies. Then switch off, so each has a turn giving and receiving the fake apology.

4. Model a sincere apology with the following 3 S's:
   - See it
   - Say it
   - Solve it

Example: "I realize that the pencil I took was yours [see it]. I'm sorry [say it]. Here, take one of mine [solve it]."

5. Have students practice sincere apologies.

6. Regroup and invite students to share how that felt.

7. Remind your students that they can recognize their mistakes with a feeling of responsibility instead of blame.

8. Allow time for your students to color in the "Apologize" slice on their individual Wheel of Choice.

The Wheel of Choice can be used in so many ways. Each student can have their individual copy at their desk. You can post a large copy on a wall in the classroom. Some schools post copies of the Wheel of Choice so large that they can be seen from the playground. Playground supervisors can carry a small laminated copy so they can intercede by showing the wheel to students who are having a problem and asking them to choose the solution they would like to try.

A fun way to distract students from strong emotions is to make a game of it. Add a spinner to the wheel and ask students to flick the spinner and see if it lands on a solution that would work for them. If it doesn't, they can choose a solution that would work for them, or they can keep spinning until the spinner stops on a solution they like.

Tammy Keces, a first-grade teacher, asked her students to pick their four favorite solutions from the Wheel of Choice and use them to make their own personal mobile. Her students drew and colored pictures of

themselves for the top of the mobile with their four favorite solutions hanging from their self-portrait.

The mobiles were hung above their desks so they could look up and be reminded of their problem-solving skills.

PEACE TABLE

Having a Peace Table, a place in the classroom where students in conflict can sit without being interrupted to work out differences, is another reminder of the importance of focusing on solutions that are respectful and helpful to everyone. Some teachers have a Peace Table with no rules. Kids in conflict are encouraged to go to the table and do whatever it takes to create peace. Some might use Three R's and an H for Solutions, the Four Problem-Solving Steps, the Tool Card Basket, or the Wheel of Choice. Others just talk until they feel peaceful—with or without a specific solution. Maybe they just gain an understanding of the other's point of view.

CLASS MEETING AGENDA

Once you have established Class Meetings, it can be simple to intervene in a problem—you need only suggest that one of the kids put the problem on the agenda (you will learn more about the use of a Class Meeting agenda in Chapter 9). Even better, you can offer a choice, "Which would help you the most, the Four Problem-Solving Steps, the Tool Card Basket, the Wheel of Choice, the Peace Table, or the Class Meeting agenda?" Actually, it's best to offer just two choices. You can decide which two seem most appropriate and offer those choices.

Young people are our greatest untapped resource. They have a wealth of wisdom and talent for solving problems when they learn the skills, and numerous benefits result when they become involved. When students participate in creating solutions, not only do they use and strengthen their skills, they also are more likely to keep to agreements because they have ownership in them. They develop self-confidence and a sense of connection when they are listened to, taken seriously, and valued for their contributions. Because they feel part of the class-room community, they have less motivation to misbehave and are more willing to work on solutions to problems.

POSITIVE DISCIPLINE IN ACTION

We adopted the Positive Discipline model three years ago in our YMCA after-school program. We were using a reward-punishment method and found that it was not creating the classroom environment that we were striving for. After instituting the Positive Discipline model, we saw an instant change in the children and the staff. We started by teaching our staff the basic principles such as body language, tone of voice, and eye contact, then slowly progressed into classroom guidelines, daily meetings, and positive time-outs. It took time and consistency for the kids to buy in to the program, but once they did, we saw amazing results.

Three years later Positive Discipline is now an essential part of all our childcare programming from ages two through eighteen, including our summer day camp. Our leadership staff is required to read *Positive Discipline in the Classroom*, and all staff are trained in Positive Discipline practices prior to starting. Every classroom conducts a daily meeting, comes up with its own guidelines, and works through trial and error to come up with solutions. We used to tell the kids what the rules were and what the punishments would be. Now they come up with their own guidelines and take ownership and pride in following them. They feel empowered and respected. The most important thing we took from the book was that we are working toward improvement not perfection.

Laura Koellmer and Geoff Malyszka,
YMCA, Wilton, Connecticut

8

CLASSROOM MANAGEMENT TOOLS

We constantly encourage or discourage those around us and, thereby, contribute materially to their greater or lesser ability to function well.

RUDOLF DREIKURS

Students learn both academic and social-emotional skills best when classroom management is based on mutual respect. This chapter adds eleven tools to ensure respectful classroom management throughout the day. As with any toolbox, no one tool is appropriate for every job; it is important to have a variety to choose from.

One school principal shared that when a teacher came to her with a complaint about a student, she would open our previous edition of this book to the chapter on classroom management tools and go through the headings, asking which Positive Discipline strategies the teacher had tried. Doing so served as a reminder that there are many possibilities for teachers to use.

1. LIMITED CHOICES

Many difficult problems seem easier to solve when choices are presented as solutions. As the teacher, you can help your students succeed by offering an appropriate choice between at least two acceptable solutions. The key words here are *appropriate* and *acceptable*.

Many times a choice is not appropriate. For instance, it is not appropriate to give students a choice as to whether they want to learn to read, go to school, hurt someone else, be in a dangerous situation such as climbing on the roof, and so on. Other choices are appropriate but limited, such as "You may read this book or this other book" or "You can do your homework during free time or at home." "What would help you the most right now—to use the Four Problem-Solving Steps or the Wheel of Choice?"

It is not appropriate to give broad choices to younger students, such as "Where do you want to sit?" or "What do you want to learn?" Younger students need more limited choices, such as "You may sit at this table or that table" or "We can do our art assignment first or our math assignment. Which do you prefer?" With older students, you can give much broader choices because their skills at making decisions and dealing with consequences are usually more developed. With young students, you might ask, "Would you like to write a report on a butterfly or a turtle?" With older students you could give a choice such as "Would you like one week or two weeks to get your report done? You pick the topic."

A choice is acceptable when you are willing to accept either option that the student chooses. Don't offer a choice that is not acceptable to you. When you do offer a choice, if the student picks something completely different, say, "That was not one of the choices. Try again."

2. CLASSROOM JOBS

Assigning classroom jobs—giving students opportunities to contribute in meaningful ways—is one of the best methods to help students feel a sense of belonging and significance. Doing assigned jobs gives students the satisfaction of contribution, and teachers don't have to do everything!

A simple way to assign classroom jobs is to brainstorm enough jobs so that every student has one. One of the jobs could be the job monitor, the person who checks the list each day to see if each job has been done. If the job hasn't been done, it is the monitor's responsibility to remind the student who forgot.

Post the list of jobs on a job chart located in a convenient place. Your list might include the following:

Make job chart	Collect papers
Pass out papers	Feed fish
Water plants	Monitor office messages
Decorate bulletin board	Decorate room
Straighten bookshelves	Restock supplies
Be line monitor	Be cleanup monitor
Empty pencil sharpener	Be lunchroom monitor
Be morning greeter	Be playground equipment monitor

A good idea is to set up a rotation system and switch jobs each week. Sometimes students will prefer to keep the same job for a whole semester. This option is okay if everyone agrees. If one person gets to have the favorite job for long periods, you might have a mutiny.

You may wish to set aside part of each day as job time so that students aren't disruptive when doing their chores. Some jobs may require training, so take time to show a student where the supplies are or how to succeed at the job. Be available at job time to help students who need your assistance.

Mrs. Petersen's kindergarten class brainstormed jobs for cleanup time and then had fun thinking up silly names for each job. The person who cleans up the constant debris of paper scraps under the tables is called the Tops and Tidy, or T&T. Each student keeps the books he or she is reading in individual boxes; the person who straightens up these boxes is called the Books and Boxes, or B&B. The person who hands out the papers or other items is called the Table Captain, or TC.

The person who sees that the chairs are pushed in is called the Big C. Mrs. Petersen reported, "The room is cleaned up so fast when I say, 'Time to clean the room now.' There are four students at each table, so we have four jobs for cleanup time. The jobs rotate each Monday.

If someone is absent, the person who had their job the week before does it and their own job also."

Mrs. Traughber's class designed an elaborate chore chart. The students used construction paper to make pockets for each job. Then each student designed a card with his or her name on it. The first task of the job monitor was to rotate the name cards in the job pockets.

Mrs. Larsen, a high school art teacher, had to miss two days of school to attend a workshop. She took a different spin on assigning classroom jobs for her absence. The day before she was to be gone, she asked her students if they would prefer having the substitute show movies or having the students run the class themselves using the teacher's lesson plans. The class was working on a mural for the school, and the students wanted to finish it on time. Hands waved as they volunteered to handle the needed activities. When Mrs. Larsen returned from her workshop, the substitute left a note saying that the students were well behaved, task oriented, and excellent teachers.

3. ACT, DON'T TALK

You can act instead of talking. Listen to yourself for one day. You might be amazed at how many useless words you speak. If you decide to act more and talk less, your students will notice the difference. Instead of asking again and again for the class to be quiet, wait quietly for them to give you their attention. Flip a light switch if it gets too noisy.

One teacher constantly nagged her students to stay away from the board when they came into the room. She tried walking over to them with her lips closed, gently removing the chalk from their hands, and softly turning them toward their desks. The students were so surprised, they sat down immediately, opened their books, and started working. The teacher was almost as surprised as they were. The teacher learned to stop saying things she didn't mean. If she meant it, she was prepared to follow through with action instead of words. Since that meant giving an issue her full attention from start to finish, she soon began to ignore minor interruptions and deal with the ones that were very important.

When children are young (preschoolers to age eight), follow-through is relatively simple. When you say something, mean it. When you mean it, follow through with kindness and firmness. Or as Dreikurs used to say to parents and teachers, "Shut your mouth and act."

Mrs. Valdez was in the habit of coaxing Jennifer to put her blocks away and come to the reading circle. After learning about follow-through, she decided on a different course of action. The next day at reading time, she went over to Jennifer, took her by the hand, and kindly and firmly led her to the circle. Afterward, just before recess, she asked Jennifer, "What do you need to do before you'll be ready for recess?" Jennifer innocently said, "I don't know." Mrs. Valdez simply pointed to the blocks. Jennifer went over to the blocks and dallied. She had about half the blocks picked up when the recess bell rang. Mrs. Valdez stopped her at the door, led her back to the block area, and pointed to the blocks. Jennifer picked them up as fast as she could so she wouldn't miss any more recess. Jennifer learned that her manipulative tactics were no longer effective. Mrs. Valdez learned how much easier and more effective it was to follow through with very few words than to use lectures, threats, and punishment.

If you think your students won't cooperate as readily as Jennifer did, don't be discouraged. If you follow the Four Steps for Effective Follow-Through and avoid the Four Traps That Defeat Effective Follow-Through, students will cooperate even when they don't especially want to. They seem to pick up the feeling that what is required is reasonable and that they are being held accountable respectfully.

As children get older, follow-through is more effective if they are more involved in the agreement-making process. The Four Steps for Effective Follow-Through describe this process.

Four Steps for Effective Follow-Through

1. Have a friendly discussion in which everyone gets to voice his or her feelings and thoughts about an issue (during a Class Meeting or during a conference with one or more students).
2. Brainstorm possible solutions, then choose one with which both the teacher and the student(s) agree.

3. Agree on a specific time deadline (to the minute).

4. Understand your students well enough to know that the deadline may not be met. Follow through with your part of the agreement by holding them accountable, as Mrs. Valdez did with Jennifer.

Four Traps That Defeat Effective Follow-Through

1. Expecting students to have the same priorities as adults
2. Judging and criticizing instead of sticking to the issue
3. Not getting agreements, including a specific deadline and a specific action the teacher will take, in advance
4. Using words instead of action

Ms. Lockner, a high school dance teacher, told her students on the first day of class that they could dance either barefoot or in dance shoes. A lively discussion ensued—the girls wondered why they couldn't dance in stockings or in tennis shoes. Ms. Lockner explained the reasons for her choice, which all had to do with safety. She understood that the girls did not want to go barefoot and realized that dance shoes were expensive, but she said that unless the girls were in proper attire, they wouldn't be allowed to dance.

Naturally, during the first week of school, several of the girls forgot to bring their dance shoes and complained about having to dance barefoot. Ms. Lockner practiced follow-through by smiling warmly and asking, "What was our agreement?" She continued to smile without saying a word as the girls argued, begged, and cajoled her to allow them to dance in their tennis shoes. When Ms. Lockner refused to engage, the girls took off their shoes and socks and danced barefoot without complaint.

Follow-through is a gentle way to guide students to do what needs to be done for their greater benefit or to maintain respect for self and others. Raising and teaching children is not easy. Using follow-through can make it easier—and more rewarding, too.

Some teachers object to using follow-through, saying, "We don't want to have to monitor students to keep their agreements. We expect them to be responsible without any effort from us." We have four questions for these teachers:

1. When you don't take time to enforce your agreements with dignity and respect, do you spend time scolding, lecturing, and punishing them for not keeping their agreements?
2. Have you noticed how responsible kids are about keeping agreements that are important to them?
3. Wouldn't you rather do something that is a priority for you than something you don't want to do?
4. What motivates you to do things you don't want to do—respect from others or disrespect? (Even though picking up blocks may not have been Jennifer's priority, it was important that she pick up the blocks.)

Using follow-through takes less energy and is much more fun and productive than scolding, lecturing, and punishing. It helps teachers be proactive and thoughtful instead of reactive and inconsiderate. It can help you empower students by respecting who they are while teaching them the importance of making a contribution to the classroom. It is an excellent alternative to both authoritarian methods and permissiveness. With follow-through you can meet the needs of the situation while maintaining dignity and respect for all concerned. Follow-through is one way to help children learn the life skills they need to feel good about themselves while learning to be contributing members of society.

4. CURIOSITY QUESTIONS

Too many teachers tell their students what happened, what caused it to happen, how they should feel about it, and what they should do about it. Instead teachers should be asking students:

What happened?

How do you feel about it?

What do you think caused it to happen?

How were others involved?

What ideas do you have to solve this problem?

These are just examples of possible questions and should not be used as a script—which would sound insincere. You can ask Curiosity Questions in many ways (unique to you) and in many situations.

An eighth-grade teacher wanted to rearrange her room. She started to tell the students what to do and suddenly realized that this would be a great opportunity for them to think through the steps on their own. She asked, "What ideas do you have for how we could arrange the room so everyone can see each other?" Five or six students had suggestions, and the class voted in favor of one of the ideas.

Out of habit the teacher started to instruct everyone on what to do and realized again that she could ask instead of tell. It took a lot longer than usual to rearrange the room, but the kids got practice in thinking and in being actively involved. Although she was aware of how difficult it is to break the habit of giving all the instructions instead of asking questions, the teacher decided it was worth working on. Her students became more engaged than usual, and they all pitched in to rearrange the room instead of leaving the job for a few regulars.

When you tell instead of ask, you discourage students from

developing their judgment skills, consequence skills, and accountability skills. You fail to give them the wonderful gift of seeing mistakes as opportunities to learn. Telling instead of asking also teaches students what to think instead of how to think, which is very dangerous in a society filled with peer pressure, cults, and gangs. Whenever you are tempted to tell, stop yourself and ask instead.

More often than not, respectful asking invites cooperation. Since most adults have more experience in telling than in asking, the following activity will give you practice in asking "what" and "how" questions. You might want to try this during a faculty meeting.

ACTIVITY: "WHAT" AND "HOW" QUESTIONS

OBJECTIVE

To experience that it is more effective to help students learn from their experiences than to lecture or punish them

COMMENT

Education comes from the Latin word *educare*, which means, "to draw forth." Too often adults try to "stuff in" through lectures, then wonder why students tune out instead of learning.

DIRECTIONS

1. Ask participants to form pairs and sit on chairs facing each other.

2. Ask participants to take turns role-playing the student and the teacher (for one to two minutes each).

3. The "teacher" starts by stating a behavior he or she has noticed (such as not turning in an assignment), and then avoids the temptation to lecture.

Instead, the "teacher" follows with "what" and "how" questions. Give the following examples:

I notice you didn't turn in your assignment. *What* happened? (Listen.)

What do you think caused that to happen? (Listen.)

How do you feel about what happened? (Listen.)

What effect do you think this might have had on others? (Listen.)

What did you learn from this experience? (Listen.)

How do you plan to solve the problem? or What ideas do you have to prevent this from happening in the future? (Listen.)

How can I help? (Listen.)

It is important for you to keep listening to your students. Too often teachers are tempted to jump in and start lecturing about something a student says. This invites the student to stop learning and to become defensive and tune out.

Usually, students say "I don't know" because they have learned they have a right against self-incrimination. It might be helpful to say, "I have faith in you that you can figure this out. I'll get back to you in ten minutes (or tomorrow morning)." Be sure to set a definite time when you will continue the discussion and then keep the appointment.

Some principals have written the questions from this "What" and "How" Questions activity on sheets of paper. When a student is sent to the office, that student is given time to reflect on what happened by answering the questions in writing. Then the principal and student can use the answers as a basis for discussion and problem solving.

A word of caution: Don't ask for students' perceptions unless you are truly interested in them and want to help them learn to think and problem-solve. Never follow an answer with a lecture. If students tell you they were angry that they didn't get a turn, it is not appropriate to tell them that they should be more patient. Either listen politely or keep asking questions that invite students to come to their own conclusions.

5. REDIRECTION QUESTIONS

One of the best ways to redirect behavior is to ask questions related to the behavior that you would like to change. For example, if the class is getting too noisy, ask, "How many of you think it's too noisy for people to concentrate? How many do not?" It's important to ask the question both ways in order to allow room for honest responses. Many Positive Discipline teachers have created a series of hand signals that the kids can use for questions like this such as thumbs up, thumbs down, and flat hands crossing over each other if the answer is "I don't know."

Asking the question is usually enough to invite students to think about their behavior and what needs to be done. When an atmosphere of mutual respect has been established, students usually want to co-operate. The question simply helps them become aware of what is needed.

Ask the question while the students keep working. No discussion is needed. It's interesting to watch how much the situation improves just by asking a redirection question. We watched one teacher use a creative variation of a redirection question by stopping the class in the middle of an activity and saying, "I just have to ask, how many of you want to help Jose with his times tables? Jose, look at all those hands! Pick someone to help you practice your sevens."

6. DOING NOTHING (NATURAL CONSEQUENCES)

Surprisingly, an effective tool for mutually respectful classroom management is to do nothing and see what happens. One eighth-grade math teacher responded to every little interruption in her classroom. She answered every question, commented on every annoyance, and spent most of her class time putting out fires and getting nowhere. When she heard about the do-nothing idea, she was dubious. It had never occurred to her that she could let some things go by, but she decided to try it.

To her surprise, students usually stopped the disturbing behavior on their own, or classmates asked them to stop. The numerous questions seemed to disappear when she stopped responding to the ones that seemed inappropriate. Later she overheard a student saying, "Don't ask the teacher. She's having a bad day. Maybe I can answer that question."

When she heard the students helping each other, she said, "I'm so happy to see how much you can handle without my involvement. I'm not angry with you or having a bad day, but I really would like to do less reacting and more teaching. How many are willing to help me out?" All the students in the class raised their hands.

7. DECIDING WHAT YOU WILL DO

Most Positive Discipline tools encourage student involvement to help them learn cooperation and social interest. However, sometimes a teacher can decide what he or she will do (instead of what students should do) and can follow through with kind and firm action instead of lecturing or punishing.

Will we ever learn that the only behavior we can control is our own? Adults may be able to make children *act* respectfully, but we can't make them *feel* respectful. The best way to encourage students to feel respectful is to control our own behavior and be models of respect, both for ourselves and for others.

An important part of respect and encouragement is honoring a person's right to control his or her own behavior. When teachers try to control students' behavior, they are being disrespectful toward students. Even though adults are often disrespectful to children, they insist that children show respect to adults. Does this make sense?

Deciding what to do instead of trying to control others may be a new idea for some teachers. The following examples should start you thinking creatively.

One teacher got tired of repeating directions all the time. She told the class that she would give directions only once and, if necessary, would write them on the board. If someone didn't understand or hear them, that was okay; that student could ask a classmate. The teacher was not going to repeat herself. Some students still came to her and asked, but when they did, she simply smiled and shrugged her shoulders. The students would either begin working or ask others for help.

The next example demonstrates a combination of follow-through and deciding what you will do. Mrs. Adams was having a difficult time with Justin, who continually got out of his seat to ask questions. Although she tried to answer his questions, she noticed he really seemed to want constant attention. She tuned in to her feeling of irritation and used the Mistaken Goals Chart (see Chapter 4) to verify that Justin's mistaken goal was Undue Attention. Realizing this helped her decide on a plan to encourage him. She said to him, "I notice you have a lot of questions. I'm willing to answer three a day. I'll hold up my fingers each time I answer one of your questions, and when three fingers are used up, I won't answer any more questions until tomorrow. You might want to make sure you can't figure out the answer for yourself before you ask me." In this way, she weaned him from seeking Undue Attention but still gave him some special attention with their private signal.

Justin acted in his old way on Monday, and Mrs. Adams followed through with firmness and kindness, and no words, after she had answered three questions. On Tuesday he came up to her desk twice as many times as usual. (At first, before they find a new way of behaving, children often try even harder to get the response they used to get.) Mrs. Adams wondered if her idea was going to work, but she reminded herself that she had decided to follow through for one week. When Justin whined because she wouldn't answer any more questions, she smiled at him and held up her three fingers. On the fourth day he came up only twice, and on Friday he said, "I think I'll only have three questions today. That's enough for next week, too."

Mrs. Adams breathed a sigh of relief. "Justin," she said, "I'm feeling much better about answering your questions when you don't ask so many. I notice you've been finding many answers for yourself. You are doing a good job."

Justin had learned that his teacher meant what she said and that she would follow through with firm and kind action. He also learned that his choices had a related, respectful, and reasonable consequence. He had a choice of asking twenty questions and getting three answered or asking three questions. He learned about responsibility. He also learned that he was capable of finding some answers for himself. One of the greatest gifts for him was that he got an opportunity to learn about treating himself and others with dignity and respect, which the teacher so beautifully demonstrated.

8. SAYING NO RESPECTFULLY

It's okay to say no. If it's all you ever say, that's a problem, but some teachers don't think they have the right to say no without lengthy explanations.

One day when a group of students was feeling especially rowdy in a sixth-grade class, they asked their teacher, "Can we take a break and play a game?" The teacher responded, "No." "Why not? That's not fair. Mr. Smith lets his class do it."

The teacher said, "Watch my lips. No."

"Aw, come on, be a sport. You're so tight."

"What part of no don't you understand?"

"Okay. You're no fun. I guess we have to finish our work."

The teacher just smiled.

Her behavior may sound disrespectful—some people have thought she should have explained her reasons. But what is actually disrespectful is to explain to students what they already know. These students knew what they needed to do and were trying to manipulate their way out of it. This teacher kindly and firmly avoided falling for the manipulation, thus demonstrating kindness and firmness for herself, for the students, and for the needs of the situation.

9. PUTTING EVERYONE IN THE SAME BOAT

Teachers often pick on one student for a problem. But it's difficult to truly know all the players involved in a situation. Pretending, or believing, that you have the ability to be judge, jury, and prosecutor all at once is not practical.

It's better to put all the students in the same boat, as in the following applications.

One or two students are whispering while others are doing their work. "Class, it's too noisy in here," says the teacher.

Someone tattles on another student. "I'm sure you two can work it out," the teacher says.

A student grabs another student's book, and papers fly all over the room. "Please pick up the papers and get back to work," the teacher says.

Notice that the teacher does not use individual names. She puts them in the same boat by addressing everyone.

Suppose the class responds, "That's not fair. I wasn't doing anything wrong," or "Teacher, it was Tom, not me." You simply say, "I'm not interested in finding fault or pointing fingers but in getting the problem resolved."

Many teachers think it's their job to fix everything and that they are the only ones with good ideas. Instead—in a variation of putting everyone in the same boat—ask those involved in a problem to figure out what to do, and then watch their creativity at work.

In one classroom, students fought over who could use the balls at recess. The teacher said, "I'm putting the balls away until all of you figure out a system for sharing without fighting. Let me know when you've worked it out, and you can try again." At first the students grumbled, but later three boys announced, "We worked it out. The kids whose last names start with A through M can have the balls on Mondays and Wednesdays, and the N through Z kids can have them on Tuesdays and Thursdays. Friday is free day. We all agreed."

In this example, if the students started squabbling again, the teacher could simply say, "Back to the drawing board. The ball-sharing plan seems to be falling apart. Let me know when you're ready to try again, and then you can use the balls."

10. POSITIVE TIME-OUT

We all have times when, for one reason or another, we don't behave at our best. Daniel Siegel, in *Parenting from the Inside Out,* calls this "flipping our lids"—when we "react" instead of "acting" rationally. Dr. Siegel uses a closed fist as a model for the brain. The fingers closed over the thumb represent the cortex—the only place where rational thinking takes place. The thumb inside the fist represents the midbrain, where old fears, including fear of inadequacy, are stored. Memories of these fears can activate the fight-flight-freeze part of the brain stem, which is represented by the palm of the hand to the wrist. (Watch Dr. Siegel demonstrate at http://www.youtube.com/watch?v=DD-lfP1FBFk.)

Positive time-out is different from punitive time-out. Punitive time-out is used when a child is sent to a time-out and usually told to "Think about what you did." Punitive time-out includes a feeling of blame, shame, and punishment.

There is no blame or shame for positive time-out. Teachers involve students in creating a space that will help them clam down and feel better—teaching self-regulation. Since time-out has a punitive reputation, students are invited to give the space a name that represents the purpose, such as "Cool-Out Space," or "Feel-Good Space," or "Hawaii." Then, instead of being sent to the positive time-out space, children are invited to choose it. One of the rules for positive time-out might be that they can go to the "space" whenever they feel the need. Another possibility is for a teacher to provide a choice: "What would help you right now—to put this on the Class Meeting agenda or to go to our cool-out space?" Creating it, naming it, and choosing it gives students ownership in the process.

Using a positive time-out teaches children the valuable life skill of taking time to calm down until the rational part of the brain is back in charge again. It is an encouraging and empowering experience for students instead of a punitive and humiliating one, and it gives everyone involved a cooling-off period.

Positive time-outs are encouraging because they let students take a break for a short time and try again once they're ready to change their behavior. A punitive time-out may stop a student's misbehavior for a moment, but the benefits will only be short term if the student decides to get even or give up. In a positive time-out, the teacher reminds the student that feelings and actions are not the same, and that what we feel is never inappropriate, but what we do often is. A positive time-out can help a student calm down until he or she feels better, because people do better when they feel better.

Teachers who are more concerned about long-term benefits than about short-term control will see the value of encouraging positive time-out. The key is the teacher's attitude and the explanation given to students.

As with most methods we discuss, it's important to get students involved. In the following activity, they help create a Positive Time-Out Area.

ACTIVITY: POSITIVE TIME-OUT

OBJECTIVE

To teach students and teachers that time-out can be positive, encouraging, and empowering instead of punitive

COMMENT

Where did we ever get the crazy idea that in order to help students do better, we first have to make them feel worse? Students (and adults) do better when they feel better, not when they feel worse.

DIRECTIONS

1. Ask students what they think is the purpose of time-out in sports. (They will probably mention things such as catching your breath, regrouping, and coming up with a new plan.)

2. Explain that everyone needs time-out once in a while, because we all misbehave and make mistakes at times. It can help to have a place where we can sort out our feelings, calm down, and then decide what to do. Explain that this time is meant not for punishment but for calming down until the person feels better. As soon as the person feels better (and he or she can decide when that is), he or she can rejoin the group.

3. Invite your students to design a positive time-out area. Since most people have a difficult time thinking of time-out as positive, ask them as part of their plan to choose a name for the area. Some students have decided to call their time-out areas the "Cooling-Off Place" or the "Feel-Good Place."

4. Have students get into groups of six. Give each group a sheet of butcher paper and a marking pen. Allow them five minutes to brainstorm the ideal time-out area, which will be designed to help them feel better. Many time-out areas include soft cushions, books, stuffed animals (even for high school students), and something to play soothing music.

5. Ask students to turn over their sheets of papers and brainstorm guidelines for a time-out plan. Tell them that some teachers raise objections: "What if students misbehave just so they can go listen to music?" or "What

if students want to stay in time-out all the time because they'd rather play with toys or sleep in the beanbag chair?" Encourage them to consider solutions to these concerns in their proposed guidelines.

6. After five minutes of brainstorming, ask each group to read its suggestions aloud. Analyze the ideas with the class to form a plan for a positive time-out area that would be respectful to everyone and helpful to those who need it.

7. Discuss with students which kind of time-out (punitive or positive) would be more helpful to them in motivating improved behavior. Why? What do they think, feel, and decide when they are banished to punitive time-out? What do they think, feel, and decide when they experience positive time-out?

COMMENT

Teachers often are afraid students will take advantage of an invitation to take a nap, read a book, or just gaze out the window. If your students do take advantage, then you have another problem that needs attention—a power struggle, a revenge cycle, or assumed inadequacy. If that's the case, you may need to follow any of the suggestions on the Mistaken Goals Chart (see Chapter 4), ask "what," "why," and "how" questions, or get help during a Class Meeting for solutions.

After you have taught students about positive time-out, you can offer it to them as a choice when they are having a problem. If a student's behavior is inappropriate (disrespectful to others), ask that student if it would help to go to the time-out area. Or offer the student several options. For example, "Which would help you most right now: positive time-out, something on the Wheel of Choice, or putting this problem on the agenda?" Positive time-out invites accountability when it is just one of several options for a student to choose.

A POSITIVE TIME-OUT BUDDY

Some teachers allow students to choose a listening buddy to go to time-out with them. After students have learned about listening skills (from the activities in Chapter 6), a listening friend might be part of the time-out plan. This means a student can choose a friend who will

go to time-out with him or her, simply to listen while he or she talks about the current problem or situation. Or the listening buddy can sit quietly and give comfort to a student who is upset. Sharing while someone listens can be very healing.

POSITIVE TIME-OUT WITH MIDDLE AND HIGH SCHOOL STUDENTS

Many teachers are concerned that older students might take advantage of positive time-out and spend all their time there. This has not been the case when students are respectfully involved in the process of creating the positive time-out area and the guidelines for its use.

One high school class designed a positive time-out area that looked like Hawaii. The whole class created a mural of the ocean, a beach, and palm trees. Students donated two beach chairs, a stuffed dolphin, and seashells.

Some teachers provide a timer for students to set according to how much time they think they'll need to feel better. Most students decide on no more than ten minutes for positive time-out. Some teachers allow students to stay as long as they need to, having faith that they will not misuse the privilege. If the privilege is misused, the problem is discussed during a Class Meeting so solutions can be found.

People do better when they feel better. We don't motivate students to do better by making them feel worse through punitive time-out. It does not help to tell students, "Go to time-out and think about what you did." It is helpful to tell students, "When you are in time-out, do something to help yourself feel better, because I know you will do better when you feel better." Oh, and by the way, teachers can take a time-out, too!

11. TAKE SMALL STEPS

Taking small steps is an important classroom management tool. The road to success is traveled one step at a time. If you set your sights too high, you may never start, or you may feel discouraged if everything doesn't happen overnight. We've discussed many classroom management tools. You may want to keep a copy of a list of tools on your desk for easy reference. Add your own nonpunitive methods that will encourage your students and promote important life skills.

The point of these classroom management tools is to teach students that mistakes are opportunities to learn, to give them life skills that will serve them when adults are not around, and to help them feel a sense of belonging and significance, so they don't feel a need to engage in nonproductive behavior.

POSITIVE DISCIPLINE IN ACTION

In my first-grade classroom, I taught the students about positive time-out and had them develop a space. They named it "The Comfortable Place." One of my students has had a very difficult time dealing with his anger. There are many issues at play for him—a tough home situation, an ADHD diagnosis. (In one episode during the first week of school, he pushed another student and shouted, "I'm going to stab you in the face with a knife!")

On Friday, a different teacher came to our room to teach a MindUP lesson. Throughout the lesson, my student raised his hand many times with an idea to share. The teacher called on him a number of times, but at the end of the lesson, she left while his hand was still in the air. After she left the room, I called on him, and he began to shout at me. I explained to him that I'd love to talk with him and hear what he had to say, but that we'd need to wait until he could speak to me respectfully. He stood up, and just as I was about to say something, (but didn't, thank goodness), he stomped off to the back of the room, white-knuckled fists pumping by his sides, shouting, "I'M SO ANGRY WITH YOU!!!" I was momentarily worried that he'd storm right out of the room, but he went to the Comfortable Place!!! He was there for about five minutes, and then, on his own accord, walked back to the rug, sat down, and raised his hand. He still appeared angry and even huffed and puffed a bit, but when I called his name, he was able to respectfully tell me that he was mad at the other teacher for not calling on him. I told him that I could understand why that might make him feel angry. I also asked him to share his thought, and he did. Success!!

Heather Ladd,
first-grade teacher, southern California

9

SOLUTION-ORIENTED APPROACHES TO BULLYING

The beneficial effects of building morale, providing a feeling of togetherness and considering difficulties as projects for understanding and improvement, rather than as objects of scorn, outweigh any possible harm.

RUDOLF DREIKURS

Hardly a week goes by without some media reference to bullying. Even though bullying has been around since the beginning of time, the media keep the issue front and center of our awareness and concern.

A concerted effort is now under way to educate parents, school personnel, and young people about bullying. This may be the result of several incidents in which students who felt ridiculed and disenfranchised killed other innocent students. Many schools have put bullying programs into place. Some of them use a punitive problem-solving model, while others teach students empowerment and esteem building.

WHAT IS BULLYING?

Dan Olweus, Scandinavian bullying expert, defines *bullying* as doing mean or hurtful things on purpose over and over to someone who has a hard time defending himself or herself. Bullying behavior is intended to hurt, and there is an imbalance of power. According to Olweus, the bully is wrong and the victim is innocent. Olweus acknowledges that Class Meetings are one of the best ways to prevent bullying, but his program does not include methods for conducting Class Meetings.

Bullying is a mistaken way of solving a perceived or real problem. It can be a long-practiced behavior of overcompensation for feelings of inadequacy. When people believe they are good enough just the way they are, they feel no need to bully anyone. But when people feel they are one down, they try to solve that problem, and sometimes bullying is how they go about doing that. Rudolf Dreikurs called it "deflating others in order to inflate oneself."

The Mistaken Goals Chart (see Chapter 4) sheds light on the purpose of bullying behavior. Some bullies are looking for attention and recognition. They are saying with their behavior, *Look at me. You can't ignore me. I'm the top dog.* We call this mistaken goal Undue Attention. Other bullies behave the way they do in order to gain power. They are saying with their behavior, *See how powerful I am. I'm the boss and you'll do as I say. I can do anything I want and you can't stop me.* We call this mistaken goal Misguided Power.

Others bully for the purpose of getting even with others or paying back others for hurt feelings. This mistaken goal is called Revenge. The behavior is saying, *I've been hurt and you're going to pay. I'm going to make you feel as bad as I do. It's only fair.* Eric Harris, one of the Columbine killers, wrote in his journal, "If people would give me more compliments, all of this might still be avoidable."*

Finally, bullying can be a way to keep others away so the bully can be left alone. Strange as it may seem, the bully wants to be left alone, without expectations for better behavior. He or she may think, *No matter what I do, it never gets better, so why bother even trying?* We can't say it often enough: a misbehaving child is a discouraged child.

THREE COMMON MISTAKES ABOUT BULLYING

KIDS WOULD NEVER LEARN HOW TO BULLY IF THEY DIDN'T WATCH THEIR PARENTS (OR TEACHERS) AND COPY WHAT THEY SEE

Parents are a child's first role model and authority figure, and teachers the next. But we need to remember that it is not what happens to and around us that makes us who we are, but what we decide about it. If aggressive behavior takes place at home or school, some young people, observing it, may decide that is the way to behave. Others may make a totally different decision, move in an opposite direction, and decide never to be hurtful or violent to others.

Some kids learn to bully from watching the media, or following their peers, or becoming part of a gang to feel safe or to fit in with a crowd. Regardless of how kids begin bullying behavior that seems to work for them, they get better and better at whatever they practice regularly. Therefore it is imperative for adults to teach children other

---

* Quoted in Susannah Meadows, "Murder on Their Minds: The Columbine Killers Left a Troubling Trail of Clues," *Newsweek,* July 17, 2006.

ways to solve problems that give them respectful way to get recognition, power, justice, and skills.

ONCE YOU DEAL WITH THE BULLY, THE PROBLEM IS GONE

Like all behaviors, bullying doesn't happen in a vacuum. In a bullying situation, there's a bully, a victim, and often a bystander. Each is affected and involved, although differently.

As you read this chapter, perhaps you've been thinking back to a time in your life where there was a bullying situation. If you haven't been thinking about that, take a minute and do it now. When you remember the situation, were you the bully, the victim, or the bystander? What were you thinking, feeling, and deciding? What were you doing? What were you wishing for? No one in that situation gets a pass—everyone is impacted, just in different ways.

If you were the bully, were you being physical? Were you threatening, intimidating, or coercing someone? Were you excluding someone or humiliating them? We're you trying to control another person or get that person to turn against someone else? Were you extorting food, money, or favors from someone? Did you gossip behind someone's back? Did you start rumors about someone? Did you decide to isolate or ostracize someone?

If you were the victim, were you smaller or weaker than the bully? Were you less popular, less attractive than the bully? Did you have a physical, religious, or cultural difference? Were you a loner? What made you a target? Did you fight back? If not, why not? Did you tell anyone? If not, why not?

If you were the bystander, were you glad it wasn't you who was being picked on? Did you intervene? Run for help? Stand up to the bully? Tell the bully to stop? Laugh? Take sides with the bully? Listen to rumors? Gossip along with the bully? Participate in isolating a person?

Over the years, Lynn has heard countless stories in her counseling practice, of folks who are still troubled by bullying situations, whether they were victim, bully, or bystander. As adults dealing with these situations, it's important that all the players have a chance to process what happened—preferably together (more about that later).

ADULTS MUST CORRECT THE SITUATION

Many families and school personnel are inadvertently doing victim-bully training in the way they deal with children when fights or bullying occurs. These adults act as judge, jury, and executioner, deciding who started the problem and punishing one of the children or labeling that child a troublemaker or bully. Adults can't possibly see or understand all the dynamics among kids, so often they end up picking on the tallest or the oldest or the male, labeling him or her as the aggressor and standing up for the child they believe to be the poor victim. They don't notice the bystanders at all. We have often seen children who are dealt with this way stuff their feelings of injustice and later explode in violent and angry behavior. They feel misunderstood and picked on, without a voice and without understanding.

In Positive Discipline we teach that everyone who is part of the problem needs to be part of the solution. The best way to implement this idea is at a Class Meeting, but even without Class Meetings, all those involved in a situation can be brought together to talk things out in the safety of a caring and neutral adult.

The history of the world is filled with stories of bullies who got their way by intimidating and hurting others. In Positive Discipline, we are rewriting that history, one family at a time, one classroom at a time, one school at a time, teaching methods that focus on respect, understanding, building consensus, and finding solutions, and that expect and help all the people who are part of a problem to be part of the solution. During Class Meetings we have heard kids come up with ways to help a child feel belonging and significance (brainstorming ways to show friendship and caring) until the bullying stopped. We have seen bystanders confess that they perpetuated the bullying situation or felt bad that they didn't speak up. During brainstorming for solutions, they agreed on methods to support each other in speaking up to stop bullying. We have seen kids empathize with the bully, getting into the bully's world through role-playing, and coming up with solutions to be supportive.

After a 2012 incident in which an elderly school bus driver was bullied, Jane Nelsen told a newspaper reporter that "the traditional means of punishment—yelling, shaming, hitting, grounding, etc.—are counterproductive." She suggested that "parents of the bullies embark on a four-step process to set aside their anger, take the time to emotionally connect with the misbehaving kids, find the reason behind the misdeeds, and then help the kids learn and grow from their mistakes"—including making amends.* The kids who bullied the bus monitor felt embarrassed when they watched a video of what they had done. They tried to make amends, but this wasn't enough for many adults, who wanted to bully the bullies and make them suffer more for what they did.

When Jane discovered that her own daughter was part of a group of kids pelting cars with oranges, she handled the incident in a way that would be appropriate to use in a bullying situation. She said to her daughter, "I'm so sorry that this happened. Tell me about it." "What were you feeling at the time?" "How do you think the neighbor felt?"

---

* Jane Nelsen quoted in Rene Lynch, "Don't Punish Bullies of School Bus Monitor, Parenting Expert Says," *Los Angeles Times,* June 12, 2012, http://www.latimes.com/news/nation/nationnow/la-na-nn-dont-punish-kids-in-bullying-video-20120621,0,7205124.story

"How would you feel if you had a new car and someone hit it with oranges?" That line of questioning led to the big question: "What do you think we can do to resolve this issue?" Jane's daughter, all on her own, came to a conclusion: she needed to apologize in person, also write an apology letter, and spend a day cleaning the neighbor's car by hand. Such consequences will ultimately teach a child why it's important to respect others, in addition to providing a deterrent.

Positive Discipline teaches that adults must work to help instill personal responsibility in children and guide those who misbehave in correcting their behavior and making repairs for their actions.

Positive Discipline does not condone permissiveness or coddling; nor does it support a sense of entitlement in children. But punishing a bully, without understanding or investigating what created this behavior in the first place, serves only to fertilize the ground for more of this behavior in the future.

WHAT CAN ADULTS DO?

Perhaps the number-one adult behavior is to *take bullying seriously* and believe that it happens and that kids need help. A lot of bullying goes on behind the backs of adults.

First, adults should be alert to the signs that someone is being bullied. A student who does not want to go to school, who does not use the bathroom until he or she gets home, who asks for or steals money or snacks (for the bully), who exhibits physical symptoms, or who tries to sneak a weapon of some sort into school for protection is showing signs of being bullied.

Next, it's important that the adults intervene. Rather than singling out just the bully, the victim, or the bystanders in a bullying situation, put all the kids in the same boat. Hold a Class Meeting, an assembly, a restorative justice circle, or a meeting with all the victims, bystanders, and bullies, along with their parents. Make sure everyone has a say and is heard. Emphasize that this is an issue for which the school has no tolerance and that there must be solutions. Remind kids that they have a right to be safe at school.

Listen to all the kids involved and make sure they have a voice. The best solutions usually come from the kids. Don't underestimate kids' creativity and ability to solve problems, often more easily and quickly than adults.

Surprisingly, the simple solutions often work best: reminding kids to walk with friends, and instituting adult volunteer patrols of halls,  bathrooms, and playgrounds. Sometimes just having an adult presence reduces bullying incidents. Help kids have a quirky comeback when they are subjected to a threat or intimidation. As silly as it may sound, when little kids say, "What you say is what you are," the intimidation often stops. Asking a bully to play ball or share a sandwich or be a friend can do wonders.

Encourage kids to put bullying incidents on the agenda for the Class Meeting. If they don't want to name names, they can put down a general item like "mean at the playground" or "stealing my lunch." Solutions are easy to generate even without naming names. Ignoring a bully can also be effective in some circumstances, taking the sail out of his or her wind. Focusing on solutions in a Class Meeting has a powerful effect on bullies. Some bullies try to save face by stating they didn't realize they were hurting others—or that they were just joking. Still, they seem to feel the power of the group members sharing their thoughts about bullying and are often motivated to change—especially when they have the opportunity to choose solutions.

It is extremely helpful to make sure your teens are part of several groups, both in and outside of school, so they always have a place to belong. Encouraging sports, dance, martial arts, hobbies, theater, and so on gives a child a different set of friends, if the friends at school decide to turn against him or her. When that happens, it's comforting for kids to know they have another group they can count on.

CAUTION: WHEN IT ISN'T BULLYING

Adults often become overzealous in their attempts to "stop" a problem. They may label behaviors as bullying when they are actually age-typical. It's very normal for kindergarten kids to taunt, "You can't come to my birthday party." We've heard of six-year-olds being suspended for "sexual harassment" or pretend-fighting at the playground. These cases are neither bullying nor sexual harassment. Young children often experiment with behavior they've heard about (on TV or from adults) that they don't really understand. Still, such incidents are opportunities to teach children that their behavior has effects on others and that they can replace disrespectful behavior with appropriate social skills. These behaviors could be put on the Class Meeting agenda so that even young children start to discuss how their behavior can hurt others—and brainstorm solutions. These kids need skills, not labels.

We encourage teachers of all age groups to do an activity with students called "Charlie." It's an activity (created by Suzanne Smitha, a school psychologist and certified Positive Discipline trainer) that's easy to do, quick, and easy to relate to. Once you do it with your students, you can use it as a reference point when difficult issues happen.

ACTIVITY: CHARLIE

OBJECTIVE

To help students see the results of cruel behavior and statements and to realize that the damage can be improved, but can't be completely repaired

DIRECTIONS

1. Draw the outline of a person on a large piece of butcher paper. Tell your students this person's name is Charlie.

2. Ask your students to share examples of comments or behaviors that have hurt their feelings. Every time someone offers a comment or behavior, crumple a part of the picture, until all that's left is a crumpled ball.

3. Ask the students how they think Charlie is feeling. Would he want to come back to school? Has anyone in the room ever felt that way?

4. Now ask what anyone could do or say that might help Charlie. When a student gives an encouraging example, smooth out a piece of Charlie until the picture is more intact. Talk about how even with encouragement, there are still wrinkles remaining. Ask the students to think before they speak, knowing that words can be very hard to take back and that "wrinkles" can last a long time.

5. Hang Charlie up in the room as a reminder and refer to his wrinkled body when kids forget to treat each other respectfully. If a student is having a tough time, ask if he is having a Charlie Day and what would help him feel and do better.

Positive Discipline has been at the forefront of providing tools to deal with acting-out behaviors (including bullying) in a nonpunitive, respectful, and effective way. During Class Meetings on bullying, students focus on a nonpunitive, solution-oriented approach—seeking to understand what happened, what caused it to happen, what each person could do differently next time to keep it from happening, and how to make amends if needed.

POSITIVE DISCIPLINE IN ACTION

I am a newbie to Positive Discipline and just started implementing it in my school in France. I started with Curiosity Questions. During recess, when the three-to-five-year-old kids fight, I ask them, "What is the problem?"

One day a four-year-old boy destroyed another kid's sand castle. The two boys told me what the problem was, and I asked them what could be a way to resolve this problem. The boy who had destroyed the castle said he could help the other boy make a new castle, and they started playing happily together.

I have also been making a Wheel of Choice. In my class we brainstormed for ideas students could do when they have a problem or a fight. They found many ideas like kissing, hugging, dancing together, talking to the teacher, but best of all—tickling! It was their number-one choice when they fought, and it always worked. Would I have ever thought of that? Never! Kids are so creative and full of resources. I am very impressed.

One of the children in the school would hit forty times a day. I taught the children how to brainstorm solutions, and the one they picked was: to tell this child that they liked him. Later in the day a student came to me and said, "Nadine, this thing about telling him we like him doesn't work well. We need to find another solution." I love it when children know we can keep looking for solutions. We had another brainstorm session to think of more ways to help the student. The kids decided to lend him this great toy car—and it worked!

Nadine Gaudin, teacher at Institut Notre-Dame,
St-Germain-en-Laye, France

POSITIVE DISCIPLINE IN ACTION

The benefits I learned from building relations with difficult students are many. I learned that some of the contributing factors that play a part in student misbehavior are their sense of self-worth, their attention seeking, and their search for identity. Students who feel they are not smart enough, or loved enough, in and outside of school, will find other ways to stand out. Students might feel that being disruptive in class is their only way to get attention from the teacher and their peers. They seek out disruptive behavior, identify it as who they are, and feel that is the thing they are known for at school. All of these factors have other factors that led to them. It is all based on how much trust the students have in coming to school, and the trust they have for the teacher. By working with these children closely, I show them that I am not going away and that I will be able to erase the students' next defiant episode. I can now respond with practical strategies that I can use in my classroom on a daily basis. Another benefit would be to empower the students. By positively changing the students' perception of authority, and discarding the type of teaching that doesn't produce long-term results, I will be able to build a trusting and powerful relationship with the students. I will also feel empowered myself, be less stressed with my job, and enjoy my students.

Loribeth Knauss, fifth-grade teacher,
Shoemaker Elementary School,
East Penn School District, Pennsylvania

157

10

TAKING THE HASSLES OUT
OF HOMEWORK

If the child is not doing well, a tug of war may ensue. The teacher may blame the parents for the difficulty she has with her students. She often demands that they exert their influence to improve the child's academic progress or deportment. Usually she gives them the responsibility to help the child with his studies, particularly with his homework. In doing so she contributes greatly to the unhappiness of the family and to the child's increased antagonism to learning.

RUDOLF DREIKURS

What's the biggest struggle parents have with their kids about school? If you guessed homework, you guessed right. This struggle starts the first time the kids get homework and continues throughout their school years, often escalating at some point to require extreme interventions such as therapy, tutoring, severe punishments both at home and at school, and even divorce because parents can't agree on how to deal with the issue.

Why does homework have to be such a struggle? Teachers mean no harm when they send home a letter to the parents. How could anyone fault the following homework policy statement: "The purpose of homework is to enhance student achievement; to help students become self-directed, independent learners; and to develop good work habits." Like many ideas, it sounds great, but is it?

In reality, even though this policy is intended to help the student be self-directed, many parents micromanage their child's homework. They want to do the right thing for their kids, and they don't want to get in trouble with the teacher. They think it's their responsibility to make sure their kids succeed, and that belief can be strengthened when teachers complain that parents aren't being responsible for managing their kids' homework.

Instead of instilling a sense of self-direction, homework teaches many kids that their homework and grades are more important to their parents and teachers than they themselves are. This hurts, so kids may choose to hurt back (even if they hurt themselves in the process) by not caring about their homework or refusing to do it without a power struggle and/or revenge cycle. Sometimes parents are dismayed to discover their kids have not turned in the homework they completed. Obviously, these kids are proving *You can't make me*.

Added to the homework challenge is the fact that kids are already busy with countless after-school activities. Parents are often working full or part time or are single parents juggling endless responsibilities. Now the parents and the kids are supposed to find time together to do homework assignments. If there's more than one child in school, it's worse. And if the teachers don't coordinate homework assignments, some children can have up to six hours of homework from six different teachers. On top of that there are those assignments that no child can succeed at without parental help.

Only rarely do teachers problem-solve the homework issue with their students. Rather, they take on an "I know best" attitude, making doing the homework a requirement for passing a class. Some kids can easily pass tests without doing homework, but they still might fail a class or be graded down for not doing it.

Having conversations with students could go a long way to resolve many homework dilemmas. Assignments could be the result of joint problem solving between teachers and students. Discussing all of this would be an excellent topic for a Class Meeting.

Many homework activities add to the richness of learning, and some help with the practice and repetition needed to learn and succeed in school. We're not suggesting that anyone ban all homework, but we think teachers need to be sensitive about the issues unfolding outside the classroom. Some children are so stressed about doing their homework, lest they get in trouble or get a lower grade, that they have no time for family activities. Others experience physical symptoms resulting from the stress. In many families, homework time is fraught with power struggles, tears, threats, refusal to do the work, and even lying, as in "I don't have any homework tonight." The joy of learning is lost when homework struggles become the main focus.

In France in 2012, a group of teachers and parents called for a two-week boycott on homework because, according to them, "It is useless, tiring, and reinforces inequalities between children." They further complained that the responsibility for homework is now the parents' rather than the child's, and that the result is endless fighting at home between the two. They suggest that if students need extra work or practice, they should do it at school rather than home.*

In one family, where the son attends a college prep private school, the parents shared that at the beginning of the school year the school sent a note home to the family asking the parents to stay out of their children's

---

* "French Parents Boycott 'Useless' Homework," Agence France-Presse, March 28, 2012, http://www.mid-day.com/news/2012/mar/280312-French-parents-boycott-useless -homework.htm.

schoolwork. They encouraged the parents to step back and let the kids figure out how to do it. They promised that the teachers would deal with the kids about unfinished homework and would work with them to encourage responsibility. The parents found it hard to let go, but the school continued encouraging them, saying that it was good practice for the kids and that they were developing skills of self-direction and responsibility. It took about six months for the new system to really work, because the old habits of both parents and kids were so ingrained. But finally the stress level around homework disappeared in the family, and their son learned to take full responsibility for his work.

In another family a mother wrote that her son started taking online classes instead of attending school. He gets all his work done during the day and can enjoy his after-school activities, friends, and family without the stress and fights around homework. This was a big change from the hassles he experienced around homework before—especially his parents engaging in piggybacking.

PIGGYBACKING

Piggybacking often happens around homework struggles as well as other discipline issues. Here's how it works: a child gets in trouble at school because his or her homework isn't complete. The teacher suggests that the parents "discipline" their child or make sure the child has "consequences" for misbehavior in school. Those are usually fancy words for asking the parents to punish the child again for something that has already been punished for at school. This is piggybacking. Imagine how you, as a teacher, would feel if a child's parents came to you asking that you "discipline" their child or give them "consequences" for not cleaning their room, or not helping with chores, or not keeping a promise to mow the lawn.

This is a two-way street. Teachers inform parents about their child's progress in school, because parents want to know how their child is doing. They don't like surprises when the report card arrives. In many cases, this situation has evolved into Web sites where parents can check how their kids are doing on a daily basis. (One parent we know of checks three times a day.) Many parents are getting an education under an assumed name—their child's.

The premise of piggybacking is that the more punishment a child receives, the more motivated he or she will be to do better. All the research shows that punishment doesn't work, yet the idea persists that perhaps more punishment will work here. It doesn't. Students end up shamed and punished first at school, then at home. The parents end up feeling blamed and expected to perform so that their child will perform. Once again the responsibility for success is placed on the parents and not on the student. In addition, parent-child relationships are impaired.

A different approach would be for parents to offer encouragement.

Teachers could simply notify the parents and emphasize that they and the student will work on this issue together at school to come up with a satisfactory solution to the homework issue. Teachers might even invite the parents in to be part of that problem solving, as long as everyone has an equal voice and as long as the adults don't gang up on the student. Some teachers put the issue of homework on the Class  Meeting agenda. When the students have input and choices, they perform better. Letting kids decide which three nights will be homework nights works much better than telling them they will have homework three nights a week.

Another option that would be empowering to students is Curiosity Questions. Either a parent or a teacher could ask, "What are your

POSITIVE DISCIPLINE IN ACTION

At the parent participation schools that I work with, the importance of Positive Discipline can't be understated. When you have adults who are coming into the classrooms to serve as parent-teachers, or as board members, or on committees, Positive Discipline is necessary as our common language. There is an understanding, in parent participation schools especially, that *the kids are easy; it's the parents who are hard.* I have been witness to things that go awry when we don't have a common positive language. Our whole school approach includes not only the teachers and students but also the families, because they are such an integral part of how our school operates.

Two important PD principles, *taking time for training* and *teaching adults what to do,* as well as using our monthly parent education meetings as Class Meetings for adults, has created a parallel learning environment for us. Parents can really get a sense of what their children are experiencing in the classroom. Creating a PD environment at school was only our first step. Providing ongoing parent education for the adults, and also making sure that, as a school, our parents are feeling *I am capable* to help, to contribute, to participate, and *I am genuinely needed* to help create a positive learning environment for all of the students, were secondary key components.

Through parent participation, we have found solutions for most of the problems that plague traditional schools due to lack of funding or staffing. Our "parent power" is creative, passionate, and consistent—we focus on solutions and find ways to get things done. Inevitably this positive discipline energy is carried over to their home life. The student's whole world changes for the better, and so does the culture of the entire campus.

Cathy Kawakami, certified Positive Discipline trainer,
San Jose, California

goals? How could a good education help you achieve your goals? If homework is a requirement for an education, how can you work out a plan for homework so that it is helping you achieve your goals?" Again, kids are more likely to cooperate when they are respectfully involved and see personal benefit.

Some teachers tailor the homework to the student. Some kids need a lot of practice; others need more challenge; still others benefit from opting out of homework by scoring high in pop quizzes.

Teachers can also set their own policy about what they will do if homework isn't completed. Perhaps a teacher could use *first this, then that*—first homework, then free time. Or teachers could recommend a homework club that takes place at school, where kids have a chance to do homework and get help if needed. Some teachers have a homework corner in their classrooms where kids help each other with their homework. Some suggest homework buddies to older students.

A fifteen-year-old reported that her teacher suggested she and another student study together for their finals. She said that on her own, she wouldn't have thought of asking someone to study with her because she wouldn't have felt comfortable. The two girls helped each other study, and both ended up with better grades than they would have had otherwise. When they were together, they studied, whereas on their own, neither would have gotten a thing done.

Students, teachers, and parents don't have to suffer to achieve academic excellence. When belonging and significance are considered as important as academic excellence, everyone benefits. When all parties practice mutual respect and joint problem solving, students do better. When the responsibility for homework is placed squarely on the child, real learning can take place. Expecting kids to be accountable instead of expecting their parents to make them be accountable produces capable young people. That isn't to say that parents and teachers can't help kids succeed with homework. When the focus is on helping those kids who are helping themselves, everyone wins.

11

EIGHT SKILLS FOR CLASS MEETINGS: PART 1

Paradise could be attained if man knew how to apply his knowledge for the benefit of all.

RUDOLF DREIKURS

There is an ongoing debate about Class Meetings among many teachers and also teachers of Positive Discipline. On one end of the continuum are those who start Class Meetings on day one and introduce and teach Positive Discipline concepts and skills step by step during this circle time. On the other end of the continuum are those who believe that Class Meetings are most effective after a teacher has spent time preparing the ground,* teaching and using Pos-

---

*The manual *Positive Discipline in the School and Classroom Teachers' Guide: Activities for Students* by Teresa LaSala, Jody McVittie, and Suzanne Smitha, www.positivediscipline .org, is filled with many more activities for teaching Positive Discipline skills in the classroom.

itive Discipline skills first in the classroom. Only then do they start Class Meetings.

Some teachers think Class Meetings are too complicated, time consuming, or unnecessary. Others believe that Class Meetings, over the long term, save them time and are the best way to help children learn the skills they need to succeed, both in academics and in life.

Of course, we are biased in favor of Class Meetings because we know children are such excellent encouragers and problem solvers when they are taught the skills and are given the opportunity to use them on a daily basis. We might give up our bias if we hadn't heard from so many teachers about the benefits they have experienced from Class Meetings.

The power of Class Meetings is demonstrated in the following examples. Frank Meder, of the Sacramento City School District, teaches in an elementary school where violence was so bad that the janitor periodically had to clean up blood. Vandalism was so prevalent that the sheriff was called on a weekly basis. Frank confessed that he got a stomachache every Sunday afternoon around one o'clock because he dreaded returning to the classroom Monday morning. At the point when Frank decided to try Class Meetings, he felt more desperate than hopeful. He doubted that his disruptive students could learn cooperation and problem-solving skills, but he was delighted to be proven wrong.

We learned from Frank how important it can be to create a lot of structure and order to Class Meetings so that the students can have the freedom to participate respectfully. He is very good at being both kind and firm. In the beginning Frank assigned seats in the circle, in order to separate kids who might have difficulty sitting next to each other. He then took time to teach them the skills for Class Meetings.

The year Frank started Class Meetings, his principal realized that although there had been sixty-one suspensions for fights that year, not one of those students was from Frank's class. She also noticed that Frank's students came to school more regularly and were improving academically. When she sat in on one of Frank's Class Meetings, she realized what a great preventive tool the meeting was. She asked Frank to show all the teachers in the school how to conduct Class Meetings.

The following year every teacher, first through sixth grade, held Class Meetings at least four times a week. Ann Platt in her master's thesis at California State University, Sacramento, reported that that year the school had only four suspensions for fighting as opposed to sixty-one the year before; and only two cases of reported vandalism, as opposed to twenty-four the year before.*

In another instance, a school had a serious graffiti problem and kept hiring painters to repaint the walls. Every time a wall was repainted, the kids put graffiti on it again. One of the teachers suggested asking the student body for ideas on how to solve the problem. The students decreed that when kids were caught writing on the wall, another student would supervise them as they repainted the wall. It's no surprise that the graffiti problem disappeared.

These teachers are just a few of the many who have experienced tremendous success by starting Class Meetings. If a teacher is willing to teach students many valuable skills, that teacher's job often becomes easier and more fun. Helping students experience belonging and significance is the most powerful thing a teacher can do. Class Meetings are one of the most powerful and time-efficient ways to teach students that their concerns and contributions are valued and that they have the ability to make a difference and feel a sense of ownership through involvement.

Even though it may be challenging at times to start Class Meetings,

---

* Ann Roeder Platt, *Efficacy of Class Meetings in Elementary Schools,* master's thesis, California State University, 1979.

we encourage you to do so. Taking the time for training is the surest route to success. Achieving proficiency in the eight skills, found in this chapter and Chapter 12, will help create Class Meetings in which students want to become involved. You have already been teaching your students about problem solving, social interest, mutual respect, encouragement, and cooperation. All these skills are enhanced and practiced during Class Meetings.

It can take anywhere from three or four Class Meetings to two months of forming a circle and introducing the eight skills to students. They won't be able to learn social and emotional skills in a few weeks. They need daily practice—just as they do for excellence in academics. If you introduce the skills gradually, students will be less restless about them and will be able to practice them a few at a time. Start by letting your students know what skills they will be learning.

The Eight Skills for Class Meetings

1. Forming a Circle
2. Practicing Compliments and Appreciations
3. Respecting Differences
4. Using Respectful Communication Skills
5. Focusing on Solutions
6. Role-playing and Brainstorming
7. Using the Agenda and Class Meeting Format
8. Understanding and Using the Four Mistaken Goals

SKILL 1. FORMING A CIRCLE

Some teachers don't want to go to the trouble of arranging their students in a circle. Some believe it won't work because kids are sitting at tables or desks. We have witnessed many classrooms in which the kids move their desks and tables to the side of the room and put their chairs in a circle in sixty seconds or less, then move them back in the same amount of time. One benefit is the amount of cooperation and skills the students learn in accomplishing this simple task. However, the main benefit is that sitting in a circle creates an atmosphere of respect when everyone can see each other and pass a talking stick so everyone has a chance to speak or pass. Some students are able to master the skill of getting into a circle in one or two tries. Others may take more time. Your students may already be proficient at forming a circle. If not, you can use this activity to give them practice.

ACTIVITY: FORMING A CIRCLE

OBJECTIVE

To create a democratic atmosphere of mutual respect in which everyone has equal rights to speak and be heard

COMMENT

An ideal way to create a respectful atmosphere is to arrange all the chairs in a circle without any tables or desks in front of them. This arrangement makes it possible for everyone to see everyone else. It also reminds students that the Class Meeting is a different and special part of school.

DIRECTIONS

1. Share the objective, and comment on it in your own words.

2. Decide whether the students will be sitting on the floor or in chairs. It is important that you sit at the same level as they are. After telling the students where the circle will be, write the following headings on the board: QUICKLY, QUIETLY, AND SAFELY.

3. Ask students for ideas about how to form the circle quickly, quietly, and safely, and write the ideas under the appropriate heading. If furniture has to be moved, be sure to discuss what has to be done under each heading to accomplish it.

4. After the students have brainstormed, ask if any of the ideas are impractical or disrespectful and need to be eliminated. Cross them out, and then ask how many of the students would be willing to follow the remaining guidelines.

5. Have students guess how long it will take them to form the circle using the guidelines. Write several guesses on the board. Ask a volunteer to use a clock with a second hand to time how long it takes.

6. Let the students try out their plan, and see how long it takes.

7. Once they form the circle, ask, "Did anyone learn anything that would help us improve next time?" Encourage students to discuss the process. Without realizing it, they are having their first discussion, which will set the tone for future meetings. Students are learning by doing, not by being lectured to, because you are allowing them to be involved.

8. Ask students if they would like to put the room back the way it was, and see if they can cut down on their time. Sit back and enjoy how much students can learn from doing something, discussing it, and trying again. Some teachers ask their students to keep practicing until they can get into the circle in sixty seconds or less.

ALTERNATE PLAN 1

An alternate way to do this activity is to skip Steps 3 to 6 and allow students to arrange the room with no instructions. Using that method, classes often end up with many different arrangements. For example, one class formed a square with the tables, and students sat on top of the tables. Another class stacked all the tables in the corner and made a circle with the chairs. Another class pushed the tables and chairs to the back of the room and sat in a circle on the floor.

ALTERNATE PLAN 2

Some kids need more order, especially in the beginning, so teachers make a seating chart assigning seats in the circle. Whether you do this is up to you.

COMMENT

Whichever option you choose, let your students be creative. If their first try doesn't work, discuss the reasons why, and let them come up with some new possibilities. This is a great opportunity for children to learn that it is okay to make mistakes and learn from them by trying again with new information.

It is important that all students, classroom aides, and the teacher be sitting in the circle before continuing. If the class decides to sit in a circle on the floor, the teacher must be seated at the same level with the students.

SKILL 2. PRACTICING COMPLIMENTS AND APPRECIATIONS

Starting the Class Meeting on a positive note is a real boost to everyone's sense of belonging and significance. Students and teachers enjoy hearing nice things said about them. Since most children (and some adults) aren't accustomed to giving and receiving compliments, we suggest using the first Class Meeting (unless it takes several to practice forming a circle) to teach them how to do it. One way to teach compliments is to ask students to think of a time when someone said something that made them feel good about themselves. Students can take turns sharing examples with the group.

Then have them think about something they would like to thank others for. Give examples. Perhaps they would like to thank a classmate for lending a pencil or helping with a homework assignment. Maybe they would want to thank someone for playing a game with them, walking with them, or eating lunch with them. It doesn't take many examples before students get the idea and can think of something they appreciate.

Junior high school students seem to find the words *appreciations* and *acknowledgments* more appropriate than *compliments*. For some reason these words seem less embarrassing to them. Here is an activity to teach compliments.

ACTIVITY: PRACTICING COMPLIMENTS AND APPRECIATIONS

OBJECTIVE

To start a Class Meeting on a positive note and to teach the important life skills of giving and receiving compliments

COMMENT

At first students may feel uncomfortable or think giving compliments is silly. If you have faith in the process and give them opportunities to practice, their skills will grow, and so will the good feelings in the classroom.

DIRECTIONS

1. Explain to students that it can feel awkward to give and receive compliments when they aren't used to it. Use the analogy of learning to ride a bike. Ask students how many of them would have learned to ride if they had stopped because it was awkward at first.

2. It helps to give students examples of backhanded compliments, or statements that might seem like compliments but that aren't really very encouraging. For example, say, "I'd like to compliment you for sharing your candy with me, because usually you are very selfish." Then ask, "What's wrong with this compliment?"

3. Spend some time on how to receive a compliment with a simple "thank you," so that the person who gave the compliment knows it was heard. When asked "What is the polite thing to say when someone does something for you?" your students will know the answer.

4. Ask everyone to think of something they've done for which they would like to receive a compliment. Allow a minute or two for students to think of something. Ask "How many of you were able to think of something?" Get a show of hands. If there are students who were not able to think of anything, ask the rest of the students, "Who has noticed something X did for someone else, or some improvement he or she has made, that deserves a compliment?" Do this until everyone has something in mind.

5. Use a talking stick, beanbag, or other item that can be passed around the circle. Tell your students that when the item is passed to them, they will share what they would like to be complimented for. Then they pass the talking item to the person on their left, who gives them the compliment. For example, Whitney says she wishes someone would compliment her on how hard she is trying not to talk out of turn. Zack, the classmate seated to her left, then says, "I would like to compliment Whitney on how hard she is trying not to talk out of turn." Whitney then responds by saying, "Thank you." Then Zack says what he would like to be complimented for before passing the talking stick to the person on his left.

6. Explain to students that eventually they will feel comfortable finding things to compliment each other for without help. Then the compliments

will feel more sincere. This activity is simply to help them get used to giving and receiving compliments.

EXTENSION: GIVE, GET, OR PASS

1. Once students feel comfortable with giving and receiving compliments, teach them that in the future they will be able to give, get, or pass. Explain: "When you are holding the item in your hand, you can either give a compliment, ask for a compliment and then quickly choose someone who raises his or her hand, or pass. In other words, you can give, get, or pass."

2. Pass the talking item around the circle again for students to practice give, get, or pass. Too many passes? Narrow the choices to give or get.

COMMENT

We have witnessed several classrooms that implemented give, get, or pass. It is impressive to witness students who feel comfortable asking for a compliment when they need one. Even more impressive is the response—so many students raise their hands to show their willingness to give a compliment to anyone who asks, even students who had not been treated well before Class Meetings were implemented.

MORE HINTS FOR EFFECTIVE COMPLIMENTS

Sometimes students like this attention so much that they take a long time choosing someone to give them a compliment. If this happens, put the problem on the agenda and ask the kids for a solution. They usually have good ideas such as allowing only three seconds. Of course, the teacher could have made that rule, but that is not as effective as turning the situation over to the kids.

At first kids compliment each other for clothing or how they look.

Let this go on for a while, until the kids seem comfortable with this level. Then let them know they are ready for the next level and teach the importance of complimenting people for what they have done or accomplished instead of what they wear or look like. You can also teach students to be specific. For example, if a student says, "I want to compliment you for being my friend," ask "What did he do to show you he was your friend?" If the student seems stumped, share an example. "I want to compliment you for walking to school with me." If someone says, "You're nice," you can help the student be more specific by suggesting that they say, "You're nice because_____" or ask the student to give an example of something the person did that was nice.

If students have a hard time coming up with compliments, remind them how easy it would be if they were asked to think of criticisms and put-downs instead. One teacher said to his class, "Isn't it a shame how easy it is for us to be negative and how hard it is for us to be positive? Wouldn't it be nicer if we had more positives in our lives? Let's keep practicing until this gets easier."

If someone gives a compliment that's really a criticism, ask that person if he or she would like to try again, or ask for help in turning the criticism into a compliment. If the person who gave a backhanded compliment can't think of a way to change it, ask for suggestions from the class. This models the helping rather than the hurting principle.

A primary school teacher helped her students learn about compliments by suggesting that students be careful not to say things that could hurt the hearts of others. The students had no difficulty with this concept and were able to share examples of how they felt when someone "hurt their hearts."

At first students may feel uncomfortable or think that giving a compliment is silly. If you stick with the activities so students can practice, the skills will grow, and so will the good feelings in the classroom. Many teachers who have Class Meetings regularly tell us that students complain when a meeting is canceled simply because nothing is on the agenda. The students suggest, "Well, we could at least do compliments."

Some teachers object that these practice compliments don't sound sincere. Keep in mind that the activities we have suggested are for practice. The awkwardness disappears and sincerity takes over as students learn the skill of giving and receiving compliments.

Some students and teachers always start their Class Meetings with compliments; others grow tired of them and start with alternate warm-ups such as sharing your favorite hobby, what you like best about school, what are you looking forward to, what is your favorite food, what is your favorite animal, etc.

SKILL 3. RESPECTING DIFFERENCES

Even though learning about differences (and respecting them) is one of the Eight Skills for Class Meetings, it is directly related to communication skills (Chapter 6). When students learn to understand and respect differences, they will find it easier to have meaningful communication with others.

It is impossible to understand human nature and behavior without understanding private logic. As surprising as this may seem, no two people look at a thing or a situation and come to the same conclusion. Have you ever compared stories from your own family of origin and felt shocked that your siblings had different memories than you about the same situation? That's what private logic is—our own unique conclusions about what is happening and what it means.

Many adults claim to understand that everyone is different, thinks differently, and has different perceptions and different goals. But when it comes to their own behavior in dealing with children, teachers often act as though all children should hear them exactly the same way, that children should understand and accept their goals and what they say in exactly the same way, and that children should all behave in the same way—obediently.

This activity is a fun way to encourage students to understand and respect differences. (Teachers might want to try this activity with each other during a faculty meeting. Not only is it fun, it also teaches them a great deal about each other.)

ACTIVITY: IT'S A JUNGLE OUT THERE

OBJECTIVES

To help students understand that not everyone is the same or thinks the same way

To teach students the importance of building a team by appreciating different strengths in everyone

MATERIALS

Pictures of a lion, an eagle, a turtle, and a chameleon (Instead of pictures, you may use stuffed animals or words on a large piece of paper.)

Four flip chart sheets, prepared in advance (Each will have one of the four animals at the top, with the remaining three in the bottom half of the sheet.)

Marking pen

DIRECTIONS

1. Hang the four flip chart sheets in different corners of the room. Place a marking pen near each sheet.

Why we want to be the lion,

Why we don't want to be

Why we want to be the eagle,

Why we don't want to be

Why we want to be the turtle,

Why we don't want to be

Why we want to be the chameleon,

Why we don't want to be

2. Tell your students that you and they are going to play a game that helps people understand that not everyone is the same or thinks the same way. It will demonstrate that there are at least four different ways to look at things.

3. Ask "How many of you sometimes think there is always a right or wrong answer? How many of you think that there is only one way to see things? How many of you sometimes feel embarrassed to raise your hand because you think everyone knows the answer but you?"

4. Show them the pictures of the four animals. Ask "If you could be one of these animals for one day, which one would you like to be?" Once students make their decision, have them divide into four groups, one for each animal. (If there is one animal that isn't chosen by any of the students, ask for at least three volunteers from the other groups to choose that animal just for this activity. Later you will be able to show how anyone can find the positives or negatives of any animal if that is their focus.)

5. Ask the four groups to go stand by the flip chart sheet for their animal.

6. Have each group choose a recorder to list all the characteristics the group members like about their animal. (These items should be recorded in the top half of their flip chart sheet.) Then have them list under the other animals (on the bottom half of their sheet) all the reasons they didn't choose to be that animal.

7. Hang the papers on the wall next to each other. Ask a volunteer from each group to read all the reasons for wanting to be that animal. Then ask another volunteer from each group to read all the reasons why other groups didn't want to be the first group's animal. Be prepared for laughter and comments from the groups, and remind students that they will all have an opportunity to share their thoughts and ideas after every group has a turn.

COMMENT

Here are some responses from several high school classes. You can use these to give your students guidance.

8. After all groups have presented their reasons, discuss what students learned from this activity. (Answers will probably include: "People see things differently," "What one person sees as a bad thing another person might see as a good thing," "Everyone has strengths and weaknesses.") Continue the discussion by pointing out that any quality can be positive or negative and that there is no one right way to be.

9. Discuss the advantages of having some of the qualities of each animal represented. Once your students have learned the communication skills and respect for private logic outlined in this chapter, they will know how to create an atmosphere of respect that guarantees effective Class Meetings. Chapter 4 addresses the Four Mistaken Goals of Behavior, which give students (and teachers) a deeper knowledge of private logic.

SKILL 4. USING RESPECTFUL COMMUNICATION SKILLS

In Chapter 6 we introduced many respectful communication skills and activities. You can review that chapter and, if you haven't done so already, use any of those activities to teach communication skills to students. Or you can teach communication skills, such as being a good listener, taking turns, and expressing oneself clearly, during a Class Meeting.

ACTIVITY: BEING A GOOD LISTENER

1. Ask a volunteer to share an interesting experience, such as a favorite vacation. Have the other students wave their hands in the air as if they want to speak.

2. Tell everyone to stop. Process with the class and the volunteer about their feelings. Ask how many would find the waving hands distracting.

3. Next have the volunteer share again, but this time everyone should use good listening skills.

4. Again, process with the volunteer about the difference in his or her feelings after this experience. Ask the other students how they felt this time and what they learned.

Whenever students aren't using good listening skills during Class Meetings, ask, "How many of you think we're practicing good listening skills? How many do not?" Students can show their answers by raising their hands. Usually, nothing more needs to be said for the problem to correct itself because the students are made aware of what they are doing from the Curiosity Questions (see page 129).

ACTIVITY: TAKING TURNS

OBJECTIVE

To avoid the problems generated by poor listening during a discussion or Class Meeting

DIRECTIONS

1. Pick an object such as a beanbag, a toy microphone, or a talking stick that can be passed from student to student.

2. When a student has the object, he or she can make a comment, give a suggestion, or pass.

COMMENT

It is empowering for quiet or shy students to have something tangible that symbolizes personal power and gives them the option to speak if they choose. Many teachers have observed that the only time some of their students share their thoughts and ideas during a Class Meeting is when they have the object in their hands.

3. Pass the object around the circle twice. The second time gives quieter students a chance to think about what they would like to say while listening to others. It also increases the effectiveness of brainstorming (discussed in Chapter 12), because a student who has already had a turn may think of another idea as he or she listens to others. It does not take as much time as teachers fear.

In the beginning some students need more guidance than others do. Guidance can take the form of Curiosity Questions: "How many of you think it's important that we take turns so everyone is listened to with respect? How many of you would like a whole room of people who can help each other with problems? How many of you think we can find solutions to problems instead of using punishment and humiliation?" The fact that students are asked instead of told and that they have an opportunity to raise their hands to show agreement gives them a sense of inclusion and ownership.

POSITIVE DISCIPLINE IN ACTION

After going through a two-day Positive Discipline training, I used the steps last year to build up to a Class Meeting for the first time. It was exciting to watch the students make decisions on their own and allow them to foster leadership in the classroom. I felt that with this program, there is a place for everyone in the classroom. I noticed that students who didn't achieve A or B grades throughout the year still felt confident in the class and that they could get help from other students. It really builds community in the classroom. It also allows each class to take on its own personality.

Julie Gilbert, Spanish teacher,
San Ramon Valley Unified School District

PRACTICE, PRACTICE, PRACTICE

Most teachers believe communication skills are as important as academic skills, yet many do not provide daily practice for students to hone these skills. Class Meetings provide students with the opportunity to practice effective communication skills on a regular basis. Teachers who have found this to be true are delighted to hear their students using their communication skills throughout the school day.

• • •

You are now halfway through the Eight Skills for Class Meetings. The last four are covered in the next chapter.

12

EIGHT SKILLS FOR CLASS MEETINGS: PART 2

The crucial factor is the shared responsibility, a process of thinking through the problems which come up for discussion, and an exploration about alternatives. Shared responsibility is best accomplished with the question, "What can we do about it?"

RUDOLF DREIKURS

The following four skills for Class Meetings focus on nonpunitive methods for solving problems. It will probably take several Class Meetings to teach these skills, but the time will be well spent when you see how capable the children become at problem solving.

SKILL 5. FOCUSING ON SOLUTIONS

The effectiveness of focusing on solutions instead of punishment now seems so obvious to us that we are baffled that it doesn't seem obvious to others. Students usually buy in to the concept of focusing on solutions immediately after participating in this activity.

ACTIVITY: SOLUTIONS VERSUS LOGICAL CONSEQUENCES

OBJECTIVE

To help teachers and students see the value of focusing on solutions instead of consequences

COMMENT

Logical consequences are often misused. Too many teachers and students try to disguise punishment by calling it a logical consequence. One way to avoid this problem is to focus on solutions instead of consequences.

DIRECTIONS

1. Write the heading LOGICAL CONSEQUENCES at the top left side of a large flip chart.

2. Ask students to pretend that two students have been put on the Class Meeting agenda for tardiness. (You might want to focus on recess tardiness for elementary school or on morning tardiness for high school.) Ask the class to brainstorm ideas for logical consequences for this problem. Record their ideas under the LOGICAL CONSEQUENCES heading.

3. Write the heading SOLUTIONS at the top right side of the flip chart. Ask students to forget about consequences and brainstorm ideas for solutions that will help them come to class on time. Record these ideas under the SOLUTIONS heading.

4. Discuss the two lists. Are they different? Does one list look and feel like punishment? Does one list focus more on the past than on helping for

the future? Was the energy different when students brainstormed for solutions than when they brainstormed for consequences?

5. Ask two students to pretend they are the ones who were late, and ask them to choose something from either list that they think will help them be on time. Which list did they choose from?

6. Ask students what they learned from this activity.

Here's an example of one classroom's answers. The first list was created by students who brainstormed logical consequences for tardy students. The second list was created by the same students who were asked to stop thinking about consequences and focus on solutions that would help their classmates be on time in the future.

Logical Consequences
- Make them write their names on the board
- Stay after school that many minutes
- Take away that many minutes off tomorrow's recess
- No recess tomorrow
- The teacher could yell at them

Solutions
- Someone could tap them on the shoulder when the bell rings
- Everyone could yell together, "Bell!"
- They could play closer to the bell
- Choose a buddy to remind them that it is time to come in
- They could watch others to see when they are going in
- Adjust the bell so it is louder

One of the many ways to teach students how to focus on solutions is to remind them of the Three R's and an H: Related, Respectful, Reasonable, and Helpful. (See Chapter 2 and also Chapter 7 for an expanded version.)

Sometimes it's important simply to trust the process and let the students make mistakes. They should work on progress, not perfection. For example, one class decided that students who rocked their chairs back onto two legs should have to stand behind chairs for the rest of the Class Meeting. The whole class agreed that this would be a helpful solution.

However, the problem was soon put back on the agenda. They decided it was too disruptive to have some people standing. They also decided to see if discussion was enough to solve the problem. It must have been, because students stopped rocking their chairs back.

TRUST THE PROCESS

When punishment is eliminated and the alternative solutions are both kind and firm, students learn to be respectful to themselves and others and are motivated to change their behavior because they experience a sense of connection. They gain courage, confidence, and life skills that will help them live successfully in our society.

SKILL 6. ROLE-PLAYING AND BRAINSTORMING

After learning the first five skills for Class Meetings, students are ready to learn role-playing and brainstorming. Choose a typical problem that you think will provide opportunities for practicing this skill, such as cutting in line or name-calling. Remind students that at this meeting, learning role-playing and brainstorming skills is more important than actually solving the problem.

POSITIVE DISCIPLINE IN ACTION

I want to share a story about a colleague, Bénédicte Amigou, who taught seven-year-olds. She had a noisy classroom and put a lot of energy into trying to calm her students. After taking a parenting class with me, Bénédicte started implementing Positive Discipline and holding Class Meetings. She has been working for eighteen years and said that that first meeting day was the best day of her career. On the agenda was how the students could get calm in the class. Bénédicte asked them how they felt when she was telling them to be calm. One said he felt like being mean to her. She said she understood him and others, then explained that they were free to talk without being judged. In the end, the students decided to have her draw a big mouth with an X across it on a big piece of paper. If they were being too noisy, all she had to do was show the picture to them. Bénédicte was impressed by her students' ideas, sharing that she would have never, ever thought of drawing this big mouth!! And it worked! The class calms down the minute she shows them the picture.

Nadine Gaudin,
a Positive Discipline associate in France

There are three main benefits to role-playing:

1. It's fun. Most kids enjoy role-playing and want to do it over and over—especially when they get to role-play the teacher.
2. It can add information and understanding to the problem.
3. It can serve the same purpose as a cooling-off period. Role-playing may diminish anger as the kids start having fun with the role-play.

ACTIVITY: ROLE-PLAYING

OBJECTIVE

To learn role-playing, a skill that can increase the effectiveness of solving problems

COMMENT

Role-playing gives students a chance to get into the shoes of other people to increase their understanding. It also creates a sense of fun that helps them be more positive during brainstorming.

DIRECTIONS

1. Choose a problem, such as cutting in line, name-calling, or tardiness.

2. Before you set up the role-play, ask how many students have role-played before. Point out that role-playing is like putting on a play, in which students pretend to be different people involved in solving in the problem.

3. It's fun to play a guessing game with the students to see if they can guess two secret guidelines for role-playing. Say, "I have two secret guidelines for role-playing in my mind. Who wants to guess what they are?" Students will make all kinds of guesses, such as "listen," "take turns," "do what the teacher says," and "use a soft voice." Acknowledge their contributions by saying, "Those are good ideas, and we should use all of these. However, the two secret guidelines I have in my mind are first, exaggerate, and second, have fun."
Students almost never guess that there could be a rule that says they have to have fun. By making guesses, students become engaged in the problem-solving process, and you get to learn more about what they think. With younger students, you may need to explain the meaning of exaggeration.

COMMENT

Because some students are victims of our society's perfectionism, you may need to give them permission not to worry about playing a part perfectly. Explain that everyone will learn more if the players exaggerate the behaviors, as a way of speeding up the demonstration of life experiences. Remind students that role-playing is an opportunity to learn and to help each other—it is not a test of perfection.

4. Invite students to help you set up the role-playing situation. Together, imagine and describe the episode in enough detail that everyone will know how to role-play the different parts. To invite them to contribute details, the teacher needs to ask some of the following questions: What happened? Then what happened? What did the person with the problem do? What did the other person do? What did each person say? What did other people do and say?

5. Once the problem has been described, ask the class to think of themselves as movie directors. Have them figure out how many players will be needed to act out the scene. List all the parts on the board.

6. Based on the description, review the lines that each player will speak and the actions they will perform. Ask for volunteers to play all the roles. It is usually effective for the student with the real-life problem (for example, the name-caller) to play the opposite role (the person being called names). Or you may choose to have the students experiencing the real-life problem to be audience members watching others do the role-playing.

7. Have the role-players act out the scene in the middle of the circle, and remind them not to worry whether it's right or not. Ask the role-player who is acting as the person with the problem (for example,

the name-caller) to first role-play the other person (that is, the person who was called names). This will give the students a chance to get into the other person's shoes.

COMMENT

A role-play does not have to last long. Some may be only one or two minutes. The role-players will quickly identify with the parts and generate feelings and information. If, after playing it out once, any changes are needed to make it more accurate, have the students try again. Most students love to role-play, and sometimes they beg to replay the scene again and again. They never tire of playing the part of the teacher or watching the teacher pretend to be one of the students.

8. After the role-play, ask the players what they were thinking, feeling, learning, or deciding according to the parts they were playing.

COMMENT

It is very important to have students express their thoughts after each role-play so they can understand more deeply what is happening. For example, if in the scenario the teacher intervened by punishing the name-caller, that may have stopped the behavior and seemed to solve the problem. But the role-player who was playing the punished student may have decided "I'm a bad person" or "I'll get even later." When you ask students what they learned from the role-playing, they may realize that they learned blame and fault finding instead of understanding and problem solving. Processing their responses can help students find solutions to problems that will lead to healthy, long-term results.

One day two ninth-grade girls had a big argument in the lunchroom. One accused the other of poking her while they were in the lunch line; the other girl denied doing it. On the way back to class after lunch, they were very angry, and the girl who had been poked threatened to "get" the other one after school, to settle the problem once and for all. The teacher wasn't sure how to handle this conflict. She had been told to allow a cooling-off period before discussing a problem, but she decided to trust the process and called an unscheduled Class Meeting. Instead of starting with compliments, she suggested that the students role-play what had happened in the lunchroom. She asked for volunteers who had observed the scene to describe it so they could role-play it.

As they listened to the descriptions, the students realized that the complaining girl who had been poked was accusing the wrong girl. It was actually her best friend, who had been standing behind the accused, who had poked her.

The complainer role-played the "poker," and the accused role-played the "pokee." Soon everyone in the classroom was laughing, and they decided they didn't need to brainstorm a solution.

Role-playing can help students and teachers see a situation from a new perspective. Sometimes, as here, they see the humor in it. Other times they see that a situation that might have seemed humorous on the surface was really not funny to everyone. In any case, role-playing can provide information that helps everyone see the whole picture.

In another example, a girl was upset with a boy who had thrown food at her in the cafeteria. She put the incident on the Class Meeting agenda. When the students role-played this scene, they loved pretending to throw food. Afterward, they were asked what they were thinking, feeling, or deciding. The boy playing the food thrower said it was fun and that he felt good because everyone noticed him. The girl playing the target of the food throwing felt upset and embarrassed and didn't want to go back to the cafeteria again. Those who were role-playing others in the cafeteria said it was fun and scary. Some were afraid they might get in trouble and wished an adult would do something. The food thrower was surprised that he was scaring some people.

BRAINSTORMING

After the students role-play a problem incident, they should brainstorm—think of as many solutions as possible in a short period of time. For the Brainstorming Activity that follows, you may want to use the same situation that you used to teach them role-playing. Then students can see how they can use the information to find a solution. Understanding feelings and decisions gives students valuable information that they can use when it is time for brainstorming.

ACTIVITY: BRAINSTORMING

OBJECTIVE

To gather ideas to solve problems without judging or analyzing those ideas

COMMENT

When students know they can present an idea without being judged, it frees them to take more chances when they are contributing, rather than playing it safe for fear of looking foolish.

DIRECTIONS

1. Use the situation that was role-played (cutting in line, name-calling, or tardiness).

2. Explain to students that brainstorming is a process that allows them to think of as many ideas or solutions as they can in a short period of time. Tell them that when brainstorming, they can think of silly or outrageous ideas

first, to start the creative juices flowing. Silly ideas often lead to practical ones.

3. Write the ideas down on the board or a flip chart. Don't analyze, discuss, or criticize them as they are coming. Just write them down, even the ideas that couldn't really work; they're just suggestions. Every idea is important, so write them all down.

4. When brainstorming is over, you will have a list of possible solutions. For ideas on what to do with the ideas, see "Choosing a Solution" on page 199.

Some students use brainstorming time to be silly or disruptive, bidding for undue attention. If you write down their ideas, without comment or emotion, you can defuse their bid. One day during a brainstorming session, a student suggested as a solution "Yell at them." The teacher ignored the suggestion and didn't write it down. The student made her suggestion again, then repeated it in a louder and louder voice, until the Class Meeting was disrupted. If the teacher had written down the suggestion right away, the student might have stopped.

In another brainstorming session, a student suggested tying a student to his desk. The teacher wrote down the suggestion without a word and went on to the next one. The student looked a little deflated because his comment didn't create the negative attention he usually received.

Rudolf Dreikurs called this "taking the sail out of their wind." Many people think that he really meant to say "taking the wind out of their sail," but think about it this way: Students blow wind (misbehave) to try to activate your sail (get you to react). Taking the sail out of their wind means that you don't react. Misbehavior often stops

POSITIVE DISCIPLINE IN ACTION

I teach in a first- and second-grade combo class. The wonders of Class Meetings continue to unfold for me. While students tend to choose problem solving for addressing their agenda items, yesterday a first grader in my class chose to have his classmates discuss his problem without fixing it. The problem had to do with bigger kids taking younger kids' digging sticks.

As the talking stick was passed around the circle, I really felt the magic of "discuss without fixing." The student who put that item on the agenda had hoped to marshal the rest of the class in a retaliatory response, but other students stepped up to explain the older kids' point of view and their need for sticks to work on their sod fort. Still others brought up that it wasn't fair for the older students to monopolize various fort-building resources (dried grass, dirt clods, and sticks). Various possible solutions were mentioned, including one that said younger students could form a human pyramid to reach a digging stick that had been put in a tree out of their reach; another suggested speaking to supervising adults. Others cautioned that retaliation might not work well because it would lead to more problems.

I sat there listening to these students and had a much deeper understanding of what it is like to be little on the playground. I was struck by the way the class was able to discuss the issue thoughtfully. They brought up so many points that I might have wanted to make. I am so glad I kept my comments short and mainly facilitated their discussion. This experience leads me to trust both the process and my students more.

Adrian Garsia, certified Positive Discipline trainer,
Santa Cruz, California

when students don't get the usual reaction. When the brainstorming was finished, the other students decided to eliminate that suggestion from the list because it wasn't respectful.

Once students finish brainstorming, you may ask them to eliminate disrespectful suggestions from the list of possible solutions. Another possibility is to see what happens if all suggestions are left, because students rarely if ever choose disrespectful suggestions. Students are amazingly good at choosing the suggestion that will be most helpful.

CHOOSING A SOLUTION

Here is a list generated by brainstorming after students role-played the food-throwing problem.

1. The boy who threw food could apologize.
2. The girl could throw food back.
3. A teacher could tell them to stop.
4. The boy could be sent to the office.
5. The girl could move to another seat.
6. The girl could tell the cafeteria monitor.
7. The girl could say, "Stop throwing food at me."
8. The girl could ignore it.
9. The girl could wear a catcher's mitt.

A volunteer was asked to read aloud all the suggestions. The student who put the problem on the agenda was asked to choose the one she liked best. She chose number four, sending the boy to the office. The teacher asked her how that would help her: "Would it make you feel good if he gets in trouble?" The girl thought about it and then asked if she could change her mind. She chose number one, having the boy apologize. The teacher asked the boy if he would be willing to apologize now at the Class Meeting or later in private. He agreed to apologize now, which he did. The boy was then asked which of the suggestions would help him the most. He said that the apology helped because he hadn't meant to upset the girl.

This example illustrates four important Class Meeting techniques:

1. Read the suggestions aloud or let a student read them.
2. Allow the student who put the problem on the agenda to choose the suggestion that will be most helpful. If another student was involved in the problem, invite that student to choose a suggestion that he or she thinks would be helpful.

POSITIVE DISCIPLINE IN ACTION

A kindergarten class used a Class Meeting to try to solve the problem of how to get more big wheels for their playground. But the problem solving came to a halt when the teachers explained there wasn't enough money in the budget for new equipment. The teachers asked me for help. I looked at the budget and came back to the class with a number they could spend on equipment. I also dropped off a catalog with twelve to fifteen pages of vehicle choices. The teachers put the catalog in the free time center, and the kids pored over it for days, finally choosing what they wanted for their playground. (The teachers helped with the math to make sure the total was within the amount budgeted.) The kids felt so proud and capable and helpful that they got to decide how the money would be spent.

Dina Emser,
certified Positive Discipline associate

3. Ask all the students involved, "How will the suggestion help you, the class, or another person?"

4. Allow the student(s) to choose the time (or day) to follow through on the chosen suggestion.

Whichever solution is chosen, it should be tried for at least one week. If it doesn't work, anyone can put the issue back on the Class Meeting agenda.

Some teachers have voiced their concern that this method lets students get away with misbehavior, but we encourage such teachers to trust the process. What usually happens is that the behavior stops. And isn't that more important than making students pay for past indiscretions?

There are several reasons why the behavior stops.

1. A respectful discussion may increase students' awareness of how their behavior affects others.

2. The students don't get the usual payoff of getting undue attention, winning the power struggle, or getting revenge. Believe it or not, students who want those payoffs value them so much that punishment is a small price to pay for them.

3. The misbehaving student feels a sense of belonging and significance after being treated respectfully by the teacher and peers. This is often enough to change the belief that motivated the misbehavior in the first place.

4. Positive peer pressure takes place when other students are trying to create an atmosphere of respect.

VOTING ON A SOLUTION

Voting is an appropriate way to choose a solution when the problem being discussed involves the whole class, such as which kind of party they want to have, or which plan they like best for handling recess problems, line problems, cafeteria problems, and so forth. Most times it is better for the class to reach a consensus in order to increase cooperation and create a win-win environment. Instead of voting, continue the discussion (maybe for several Class Meetings) until everyone agrees on the solution.

Allowing students to choose the suggestion they think will be most helpful increases their accountability and responsibility. Asking them "How will the suggestion help you, the class, or another person?" encourages them to think of long-term results. Role-playing and brainstorming for solutions are valuable social and life skills that will increase socially acceptable behavior in the classroom—and in future relationships.

SOMETIMES DISCUSSION IS ENOUGH

Sometimes role-playing and brainstorming aren't necessary for solving a problem. Don't underestimate the value of a simple discussion. Discussing an issue gives students a chance to voice their opinions, share their feelings, and offer suggestions. Students who are actively involved in a respectful discussion seem to hear each other better than they hear lectures from teachers or accusations from each other. Their comments and suggestions can be both amusing and irritating—often they say the same things you've said, which went in one ear and out the other. You can choose to feel frustrated and discounted by this or be grateful that students listen to each other and come to your conclusions—or to even better ones.

SKILL 7. USING THE AGENDA AND CLASS MEETING FORMAT

Let your students know that you will set up a notebook, or a clipboard, or a corner of the blackboard, or an agenda box for items for the Class

Meeting agenda. These are problems or issues that you or the class can discuss at the Class Meeting. The whole class will join in the process of looking for beneficial solutions and will choose the one they think will help the most.

If a student comes to you complaining about another person in the class, say, "That's something we can talk about at the Class Meeting, unless you see another solution that would work for you. If you would like to bring up the item at our Class Meeting, would you please add it to the agenda?" This approach serves two functions: it saves time (you don't have to deal with every problem), and it gives the students real problems to solve at the meeting.

The only items that will be handled at the meeting are those that were put on the agenda in advance. This will allow some cooling-off time to pass before items are discussed. And just having a problem on the agenda effectively provides some satisfaction until it is dealt with at the meeting.

When teachers first introduce Class Meetings, they sometimes opt to use a shoebox for collecting agenda items. The anonymity helps alleviate the problem of retaliation, as no one can see their name on the agenda items. For writing down agenda items, some teachers put out green paper on Mondays, blue paper on Tuesdays, yellow paper on Wednesdays, and so forth, so that at the meeting the problems can be dealt with chronologically.

Over time students will comprehend fully that the purpose of Class Meetings is to help them, not to hurt them or get them in trouble. Let students know that a person's name appearing on the agenda does not mean he or she is in trouble. Eventually, students will understand that having their names on the agenda is a nice experience. They won't mind having their names on an openly visible agenda, like a notebook.

Some teachers ask students to put problems on the agenda without names so they can work on general solutions. This is fine in the beginning. However, students will soon learn that they won't get into trouble for problems, and that every problem is an opportunity to learn and to help each other. That will increase accountability.

Students and teachers can write their agenda items at any time during the day. If students congregate and linger around the agenda to the point that it becomes disruptive, put that very problem (disruption using the agenda) on the agenda. At the Class Meeting have students determine specific agenda-setting times, such as just before leaving the room for recess or lunch.

One teacher complained that her "special education" students couldn't wait to have their problems solved. Many of her students would come into the classroom all riled up after recess and need immediate attention to calm down. She tried having the kids put their problems on the agenda when they returned from recess. Later she reported that it was almost comical the way they would stomp over to the agenda notebook and angrily scribble their problem, then walk away looking smug and calm. The agenda provided immediate gratification because they knew their problem would be discussed later.

When Jane was an elementary school counselor, the teachers often called her the *broken record* because when they would ask her how to solve a problem, she would often say, "Put it on the agenda and let the kids come up with a solution"—and they usually did.

Having an item on the agenda often starts the problem-solving process before it comes up during a Class Meeting. By that time, students will often say, "That's already been solved." If it seems appropriate, ask if they would like to share how it was solved.

THE CLASS MEETING FORMAT

After introducing your students to the agenda, share the Class Meeting format as a way to provide structure and order for all the skills they have learned. Copy the Class Meeting format onto a large poster, and hang it conspicuously in the room.

Class Meeting Format

1. Compliments and appreciations
2. Follow up on prior solutions
3. Agenda items—choose from one of the following:
    a. Share feelings while others listen

    b. Discuss the problem without fixing

    c. Ask for problem-solving help
4. Future plans (field trips, parties, projects)

1. COMPLIMENTS AND APPRECIATIONS

By now the students have learned this skill. Go around the circle once using the talking stick, as described on page 175.

2. FOLLOW UP ON PRIOR SOLUTIONS

Take a few minutes to allow students to share how a previous solution is working. Occasionally, a student may share that the solution is not working. This is not the time to work on the problem again. Ask the student if he or she would like to put it on the agenda again, or try another problem-solving method such as the Wheel of Choice, the Peace Table, or the Four Problem-Solving Steps.

3. AGENDA ITEMS

When an item comes up on the agenda (in the order it was placed there), it is helpful to give students a choice. Would they like to (1) share feelings while others listen, (2) discuss the problem without fixing, or (3) ask for problem-solving help? They usually choose number three, but it's good for them to know that sometimes a problem seems to solve itself just because people know how you feel or when you simply discuss it so people are more aware of it.

One eighth-grade teacher had her students for only a forty-five-minute block of time each day. However, she believed that Class Meetings were so important that her students would have them for the last ten minutes of every class. She alternated between compliments one day and problem-solving the next, since ten minutes was not enough time for both.

Students' toothpick chewing annoyed this teacher. She had tried lecturing, scolding, and pleading, but their toothpick chewing continued. Finally, she put the problem on the agenda. When it was her turn, she asked for problem-solving help. She said, "I know this isn't a problem for you, or you would stop. It is a problem for me, and I would really appreciate your help. During the first ten-minute slot, you did not come up with a solution—or during the second ten-minute slot. On the third day (they had been skipping compliments while they worked on this issue), one student said, "Have you noticed anyone chewing toothpicks lately?" The teacher thought about it and had to admit, "No, I haven't." The student brilliantly suggested, "Then maybe the problem is solved." All the teacher could say was "Thank you all. I really appreciate your help."

In this case, even though the teacher asked for problem-solving help, it turned out that discussion was enough. Of course, it didn't hurt that she claimed the problem as hers instead of scolding the students for "their" problem.

4. FUTURE PLANS (FIELD TRIPS, PARTIES, PROJECTS)

The more the kids are involved in planning future events, the better things go. Use the talking stick and go around the circle twice for kids to share their thoughts and feelings. Be clear with students about the school requirements for extracurricular activities, including chaperones, hours, number of allowed activities, and any other requirements.

SKILL 8. UNDERSTANDING AND USING THE FOUR MISTAKEN GOALS

Most students are quick to understand the Four Mistaken Goals and seem relieved to understand what is going on for them and others. If you have used the activity on page 66 in Chapter 4 to teach your students about the Four Mistaken Goals and about encouragement, they may want to identify the mistaken goal after role-playing. Some schools post Mistaken Goals Charts in each classroom, and the kids are able to identify the discouragement of a classmate and quickly recommend a way to encourage that person.

• • •

You and your students have now learned all of the Eight Skills for Class Meetings. Likely you already use many of them throughout the day and know from experience the value of these social and emotional skills in enhancing the quality of life—and academic learning.

13

QUESTIONS AND ANSWERS ABOUT CLASS MEETINGS

Making mistakes is unavoidable, and the mistake is less important in most cases than what the individual does after he has made the mistake.

RUDOLF DREIKURS

As you experience Class Meetings, many questions will arise. Here are answers to some of the questions most frequently asked by hundreds of teachers. Some questions are from elementary school teachers, and some from junior high and high school teachers. Even though students of different ages have developmental differences, there are also many similarities. Teachers of all grade levels will find creative ideas for solving problems in the answers. Watch for the basic principles of respect and empowerment in them. Hearing about solutions based on dignity and respect will stimulate your own creativity for empowering students—and yourself.

QUESTIONS FREQUENTLY ASKED BY ELEMENTARY SCHOOL TEACHERS

Q. How do I avoid having students humiliated at a Class Meeting?

A. It is important to guide students away from any suggestions that would humiliate or hurt another student. Asking several questions helps:

How would that be helpful for this person?

How would you feel if that suggestion were given to you?

Is that humiliating or respectful?

Does that punish for past behavior or encourage change for future behavior?

Is the solution related, respectful, and reasonable?

You might wait until all the suggestions have been made and then go over the list and ask the students which should be eliminated because they are not respectful, helpful, or practical. Humiliation and punishment can be avoided by having the student with the problem choose the solution that would be the most helpful. Sometimes students do choose punitive solutions for themselves. To help them get out of the punitive mentality, you might ask, "How will that help and encourage you?"

Another way to avoid humiliation is by generalizing, or talking about the issue in general terms instead of using a specific person's name or situation. Suppose, for example, that during the meeting someone accuses another person of stealing. This issue might be generalized by asking the class, "What can we do to deal with the problem of stealing in general instead of looking for blame and trying to corner one person?" Then brainstorm solutions.

Another way to handle a situation in which humiliation is taking place is to ask redirection questions: "How many of you would feel helped if you were in Johnny's place right now? How many of you would not?" "How many of you would feel ganged up on? How many would not?"

You will need to use generalization and redirection less often once students catch on to the spirit of helping rather than hurting or punishing one another.

Q. Don't students get resentful when they ask for help and you tell them to put it on the Class Meeting agenda instead of helping them right away?

A. Actually, most students feel immediate relief just by getting their problem on the agenda. Some do feel resentful because they are used to getting special attention from the teacher. Others are used to being taken care of instead of participating in the helping process. Change, even for the good, is not always easy. Some students may feel resentful at first. But once they experience the positive attention and help they can receive during Class Meetings, which is usually much more creative than the help they receive from teachers, they will more than likely forget their resentment.

A second-grade student complained to her teacher, Mrs. Binns, that some boys sitting behind her on the bus were kicking her seat. At Mrs. Binns's suggestion, the girl put the problem on the agenda and at the meeting asked her classmates for help. The first suggestion was profoundly simple: "Sit behind them." A creatively complicated suggestion was "Get on the bus and put your books in one seat, then sit in another seat. When the boys sit behind you, you can move to the seat where your books are." There were many other suggestions, but the student chose the suggestion to watch where the boys sat and sit far away from them.

Q. How many items should one student be allowed to put on the agenda per meeting?

A. Put this question on the agenda and ask your students. One teacher had been allowing two or three items per person each day, and the issues were endless. The teacher put the question on the agenda, and the students decided on the rule of one item per person each day. There hasn't been a problem since they discussed the issue and made the decision.

Q. What do you do if a student won't pick a solution?

A. One possibility is to ask the whole class if it would be okay to see if the Class Meeting discussion is enough to motivate change. If not, the student with the problem can put the problem back on the agenda and try again.

Still another possibility is to ask the reluctant chooser if he would be willing to think about it, find his own solution, and report back to the class tomorrow. If he still seems reluctant, ask if he would like to choose two classmates to brainstorm with him during recess. Once students make the shift to understanding that Class Meetings are not punitive, they are rarely reluctant to choose a suggestion that is truly helpful. Once students have been taught the skills for solving problems, teachers need to display persistent faith in their students' abilities to find solutions.

QUESTIONS FREQUENTLY ASKED BY JUNIOR HIGH AND HIGH SCHOOL TEACHERS

Q. When students sit next to their friends at the Class Meeting and create a lot of disturbance, is it okay to move them apart?

A. This problem comes up frequently. Mr. Burke noticed his students had a difficult time being respectful when friends were sitting next to each other. He tried lecturing them about being inconsiderate. When that didn't work, he decided to separate the friends. The kids responded with hostility and resistance to the whole idea of Class Meetings.

Mr. Burke decided to put the problem on the agenda. During a Class Meeting, he asked his students the following questions and got the following responses.

1. What problems do you think we might have when friends sit together? The students brainstormed the likely problems, such as talking, giggling, and passing notes.
2. What suggestions do you have for solving these problems? The students agreed to be respectful so they could have the privilege of sitting with friends.
3. What would be a related, respectful, and reasonable solution if people don't keep their agreements to be respectful while sitting with a friend? The students decided that being separated from their friends for the rest of that meeting would solve the problem.

Predictably, nothing was effective until the students became involved in the problem-solving process. Although students often come to the same conclusions that teachers try to impose on them, the results are completely different.

Q. Are sixth graders too immature for Class Meetings? The kids in my class act silly, make fun of each other, and sometimes act like jerks to each other.

A. Developmentally, sixth graders are beginning to respond more to peer influence than to adult influence. They also want to fit in with their classmates, so if negative behavior gets started, it may be difficult to stop.

Students sometimes act silly because teachers start holding Class Meetings before they teach the students the skills. One teacher who was having difficulties told her students that she had made a mistake by starting Class Meetings without teaching more skills. After two months of not doing much more than forming a circle, teaching basic skills, and exchanging compliments, the students settled down and were ready to use problem-solving skills.

Q. If the students are uncomfortable or embarrassed exchanging compliments, is it okay to skip that part of the meeting?

A. We think the compliment process is extremely important and not an option. Students and adults alike will overcome the embarrassment stage of giving and receiving compliments when they stick with it. Variations are okay, however, as long as the opening activity is positive and results in students learning more about each other so that they can begin to give compliments.

One possibility is to ask a question about the students' outside interests, special hobbies, or other personal information. One teacher has a special book with inspirational thoughts for the day. She passes it around the Class Meeting and lets each student respond personally to the messages.

A high school teacher was teaching advanced physics to a group of students who had the reputation of being "nerds" and "brains." He told us, "If compliments are all you do, Class Meetings are worth it. Take as long as you need. The kids in my class get so much negative criticism that the compliments part of the Class Meeting was the first time some of them heard anything positive about themselves at school."

Q. Any ideas for handling backhanded compliments?

A. A simple way to handle a backhanded compliment is to say, "Oops, is that a compliment or an agenda item?" Another question that helps redirect a backhanded compliment is "Would you please rephrase that until it sounds like something you would like to hear?"

Q. I'm a resource teacher and have small groups of children for short periods at a time. I don't have time for Class Meetings.

A. There are two things you could try when problems arise in your classes. One is to ask a volunteer to put the problem on the homeroom agenda and to let you know the suggestions that were brainstormed to solve the problem. Another possibility is to conduct a five-minute Class Meeting when a problem arises. When students and teachers are well trained in the Class Meeting process, short meetings can be held in special classes where regular meetings are not held. However, short meetings do not work when teachers and students are not familiar with the process.

Q. Sometimes junior high and high school students feel like they're "ratting" when they bring up problems about other kids. How do I address this problem?

A. It helps to talk about how the Class Meeting is an alternative to suspensions and other unhelpful, punitive approaches. Remind students that it's normal to feel reluctant to "rat" on someone in a system that focuses on blame and punishment instead of accountability and solutions. Ask, "How many of you would want your name on the agenda if you knew people would gang up on you and try to get you?" Then ask, "How many would want your name on the agenda if you knew you would be getting thousands of dollars worth of valuable consultation from your peers that would be encouraging and empowering?"

Q. I've noticed a lot of complaints from students about other teachers at our school who are unwilling to hold Class Meetings. How do I handle this without making the other teachers look bad?

A. If students have complaints about teachers who won't resolve issues respectfully with them, it's important to help them do what they can to take responsibility in solving their own problems. Remind them that it is not possible to change others; we can only change ourselves. If other teachers are willing, they could attend your meeting as guests to help work on a problem.

It helps to train all the faculty in a school about Class Meetings and their potential. Remind teachers that human growth is about learning, and learning isn't smooth. The ultimate goal is to talk things over respectfully and solve problems. The fringe benefit is that classes that hold regular Class Meetings have fewer discipline problems and improved positive motivation. The more preparation the staff has ahead of time, the better they do with Class Meetings.

Q. Do I really need an agenda?

A. Yes. The agenda serves as a powerful, symbolic message that all students have the opportunity to voice their concerns while giving and receiving encouragement and practical help. The agenda also provides order and structure. It is usually not effective to try to solve a problem at the time of conflict. The agenda gives students a cooling-off period. The agenda also keeps you out of the middle. As we've mentioned before, as issues come up during the week, ask students to put the issues on the agenda.

Q. What if students choose a poor solution?

A. If the class agrees on a solution and later realizes it was a mistake, bring it up at the next meeting and work out another solution. On some occasions you may say, "I can't live with that one." It's best to avoid saying this often. Instead, let the kids learn by trying out a "bad" suggestion (if it isn't humiliating to another student) for a day or a week, then discover for themselves that it's not reasonable or workable. They learn so much more that way. Another possibility is to role-play the chosen solution, asking the players if they think it would really help after they've had a chance to see it in action.

Q. What are some of the most common problems found on the agenda at the high school level?

A. Usually, at the high school level, the Class Meeting is used to solve problems between teachers and students. Students really appreciate the chance to give input and work with the teacher on a solution. Some of the most common agenda items are (1) seating arrangements, (2) homework on weekends, (3) getting off task (the teacher usually brings this one up), (4) too much talking, (5) having a hard time paying attention to the teacher after working in small groups, (6) wasting time, and (7) students not showing respect for others.

The specific problem is not of primary importance. Problems provide the opportunity to develop problem-solving skills in a nurturing atmosphere that empowers them with the courage and confidence they need to be productive, contributing, and happy citizens of the world. Remembering this long-range perspective will help you to avoid feeling discouraged by the ups and downs of Class Meetings. You may have a lousy Class Meeting one week and a great one the next. Isn't that what life is all about? What better way to teach kids effective ways to handle their own lives?

SUMMARY OF A QUESTION AND ANSWER SESSION

The following partial transcript of a question and answer session comes from an all-day in-service workshop for five hundred teachers in Charlotte, North Carolina. As part of this workshop, first-grade teacher Janice Ritter and fourth-grade teacher Kay Rogers answered questions about Class Meetings.

PRESENTER: Today, I have with me two teachers from Sharon School. I'd like them to tell just a little bit about their experience.

JANICE: Last year, when we started Class Meetings, my initial reaction was, "Well, this is a terrific idea, but it's not going to fly with first graders." I didn't think they could even come up with a compliment, let alone solve problems. I went ahead anyway and began the Class Meeting process the first week of school, and by December I said, "This is the most wonderful thing that has ever happened to me as a teacher and for the students."

I would like to share a few reasons why I like using Class Meetings. First of all, you have more children telling you what is going on in your classroom. Also, children sometimes take things said by a peer a lot better than they'll take it from you. Children can say things to each other in a way that reaches children. Adults don't do that very well. I also like the academic skills that grow out of Class Meetings.

PRESENTER: I hope you all heard that. Say that again.

JANICE: The academic skills. As beginning writers, students love to go to that agenda, and it helps their writing skills. I have children who speak in a whisper all day long except when they have something they want to say at the Class Meeting. Probably the reason I like it the best is because behavior improves.

PRESENTER: A lot of teachers start Class Meetings to help with discipline problems and to improve behavior. That is an extremely valid reason. However, behavior improvement is a fringe benefit. The main benefit is that it teaches children the Significant Seven (see Chapter 1). That's the foundation that will help students improve their behavior not only now but also throughout their lives.

KAY: When our school psychologist gave me a copy of *Positive Discipline* and wanted me to implement Class Meetings, my initial reaction was "Oh no. This is another program that I'm going to have to read, and it's not going to work." There's no one here who could have a more negative attitude than I did. I decided to try it anyway, and after one week I was sold.

PRESENTER: You didn't have a whole month of hell?

KAY [LAUGHING]: No. After one week of Class Meetings, it was just wonderful. What it did for me was take care of little nitpicky things that drive teachers crazy. The kids would come to me and say, "Somebody hit me," "Somebody touched me." I would say, "Put it on the agenda." That was what made it worthwhile for me in the beginning. We have worked with Class Meetings and improved upon them. I have a student teacher who began introducing the idea of Robert's Rules. Not only are students learning problem-solving skills, they're also learning skills that will help them with student government. This has been a tremendous fringe benefit, as well as improving the discipline within the classroom.

PRESENTER: I heard that the year before you learned about Class Meetings, you were asking the psychologist for a lot of help with problem behaviors. She told me she never hears from you anymore and that when she asks if you need anything, you tell her you and the kids are working things out together.

KAY: That's true.

PRESENTER: Kay and Janice will now help me answer some of the questions that were turned in by the faculty members from each school.

Q. Should we post rules in our classroom? And if so, should these be teacher rules, student rules, or a combination of both?

KAY: At the beginning of the year my students and I worked out our own rules together in the classroom. Our school has school-wide rules, which are also posted in our classroom. They [the school-wide rules] were rules that the student council had come up with.

PRESENTER: What did you find when you asked the kids to come up with rules?

JANICE: My students came up with pretty much the same things adults would come up with.

PRESENTER: That's so interesting. I've never been in a classroom yet where there weren't rules posted. But usually they're all neatly printed out by the teacher in advance, so there's no ownership by the kids. What we have found is that the kids will either come up with the same rules or even tougher rules, but they have ownership, and you can label them "We decided" instead of "I decided."

Q. Should a kindergarten Class Meeting include an agenda?

PRESENTER: We had an experience in Elk Grove School District where a group came to visit Project ACCEPT.* They were writing

---

* Project ACCEPT (Adlerian Counseling Concepts for Encouraging Parents and Teachers) was a federally funded project directed by Jane Nelsen. It sought to improve student behavior by training significant adults (parents and teachers) to use Adlerian/Dreikursian

a project on decision making and had decided it wasn't possible for kids to get involved in decision making until they were in the second grade. But they watched our kindergarten and first-grade classes and were amazed. They said, "We've got to go back and rewrite the project." Many kindergarten teachers are relieved not to have to deal with tattletale issues. They just say, "Put that on the agenda." Pretty soon the kids get tired of that broken record, so they just ask the teacher to put it on the agenda. Half the time they can't remember what their problem was by the time their name comes up on the agenda.

In kindergarten or first grade, it might be okay for children to forget their problems, because once they've had a little time to cool off, it doesn't really matter anyway. But you don't want them to forget too many of their problems, or they won't have the opportunity to work on problem-solving skills.

Q. What do you do when the compliments get monotonous? For example, "I want to compliment you for being my friend" or complimenting the same person every day.

JANICE: I've done a few things. It happened in the beginning of this year—the compliments were getting very stale. So one day, instead of doing compliments, I said, "Today we're going to tell everyone one thing that we're working on." They went around the room and came up with some really good things that they were working on. Whether it was their penmanship or not to talk

methods with children. The main focus for teachers was the use of Class Meetings. Parents attended parent study groups. After three years of developmental status, the project achieved exemplary status and was awarded dissemination funds for three years. During this three-year period, school districts throughout California used adoption funds for training with their school faculties and parents.

so much, the rest of the children now had specific things to look for. I don't have to do it that often, but sometimes I find the need to do something like that.

KAY: I find in the older grades that the compliments don't get as stale as often as they do in the lower grades. Students begin to look for academic achievements and socialization skills. I found it helps to pair students. When they sit in pairs, one partner can see what the other partner does.

PRESENTER: Let me see if I understand. They have partners, and they look for things they can compliment their partner on? Do you ever have them change partners?

KAY: Oh, yes! They send their request in writing to me, and every Tuesday is Changing Partners Day.

PRESENTER: What a great idea! This also answers the question about what to do if they're always complimenting the same kid all the time. That's really nice. I hadn't heard of that one before. One that I had heard of is teachers who have kids draw a name out of a hat for a whole week. But I even like this one better. Do they sit by that person for a while?

KAY: They sit by that person for a week.

PRESENTER: Another possibility is to let them get monotonous at first because they're learning the skill. Once they feel comfortable saying, "I want to compliment him for being my friend," you can start teaching them other things. It helps to look for what a person does—their actions. For example, what do they do to demonstrate their friendship? What specific action would you like to thank them for?

Q. First-grade students seem only to make suggestions that they've heard before. How can we get first-graders to develop solutions that are more appropriate? Are they developmentally ready to create solutions?

JANICE: With my first graders I usually take four suggestions for solutions, and we just talk about those.

PRESENTER: Because your kids are coming up with so many, you have to limit it?

JANICE: Yes, more or less, and that's what they can work with. We talk about whether the solutions are appropriate and how they would work to help people. I think you will find a few students who are going to come up with the same suggestions, but you'll have more suggestions once you get started. You will probably see more problem-solving skills developed.

PRESENTER: Part of patience is allowing time. At first the teacher may have to come up with a few suggestions, but the more you learn to keep still and go all the way around the circle, the quicker they're going to start learning what great wisdom and what great ideas they do have. I've found that four-year-olds at family meetings come up with great solutions and great ideas. It's just that we haven't allowed them enough training and experience to know that they can come up with ideas. We're so used to telling kids instead of asking them.

Q. How can we make Class Meetings more than tattletale sessions? It seems that many children thrive on the attention given to them during the session.

PRESENTER: One possibility is to change our feelings about what is a tattletale. What may seem like just tattling to us can be a real problem to students. If we see their concerns as an opportunity to work on solutions instead of tattling, it puts a whole different feeling on their concerns. Usually, tattling is "I want you to punish them" instead of "This affects me, so how can we solve the problem?" Sometimes teachers like to censor items too much.

Q. What should I do when the same problems come up over and over?

PRESENTER: Sometimes teachers decide "Well, we've already talked about a problem like that, so let's not do it again." That's missing the whole point of the process of Class Meetings. The fact that Billy hit Janey is not the same to Susie when Dick hits her. You just keep letting them work on solutions. They'll either get better at coming up with the same solution or they'll come up with different ideas. But the main thing is that they feel listened to, they feel taken seriously, and they use their skills. As long as it affects them, keep letting them work on solutions.

KAY: I've also found that they come up with different solutions for different children, because what works for one doesn't work for all. My students are really beginning to look at the individual rather than just at the problem, or to say, "We've already discussed it." They begin to look at what will be effective for this person.

PRESENTER: I'm so glad you said that. That is such an important point! People are unique. They're individuals. What works for one may not work for all. One of the things kids learn in Class

Meetings is that people think differently. They feel differently. They have different ideas. They're not all the same. And so we start learning to respect differences. [See Chapter 6.]

Q. What provisions are made for children with severe discipline problems, children with special needs?

KAY: In the two years that I've used Class Meetings, if I have any discipline problems, I handle them right there. Fortunately, since I've started Class Meetings I've not had any severe problems.

PRESENTER: Did you think you had severe problems before you had Class Meetings?

KAY: Yes, and I'm sure I would be having them now if I weren't doing Class Meetings. That's one reason I'm so thrilled with Class Meetings. With the help of the students, we work most things out in our classroom.

JANICE: I find the same to be true for me. And I think there are still certain things that you as a teacher have to react to, or if you have a severe discipline problem, maybe you need to refer that child to the proper channels. You would still have to do that even though you're implementing Class Meetings and trying to solve most of your problems.

PRESENTER: I would like to make just a couple of comments about this. I want to tell you two stories. One is a story about a second-grade boy I'll call Stephen. Because Stephen was a foster child, the teacher asked for help from the Foster Youth Office where I worked. She described Stephen as "a severe discipline problem."

His classmates were complaining about all the things he did. I strongly believe that Class Meetings work, no matter what the severity of the behavior. I knew the best way to help this child was through Class Meetings, but this teacher didn't know how to do Class Meetings. I thought, okay, we'll accomplish two things at once. We'll help this child, and we'll teach the Class Meeting process to the teacher.

I went into the classroom to demonstrate the Class Meeting. One rule for Class Meetings is that usually you do not talk about a child unless that child is there. Once you learn that Class Meetings can be done in a positive, helpful, encouraging, empowering way, then it's safe for kids to talk about anything together. However, in this case I knew these kids hadn't learned to help each other yet. I knew they'd still have the mentality of ganging up and punishing, so we asked Stephen to leave the room.

The first thing I asked the kids was "What kind of problems are you having with Stephen?" They listed many complaints. I asked, "Do you have any idea why Stephen might do these things?" They said, "Because he's a bully. Because he's mean." Finally, one little kid said, "Maybe it's because he's a foster child." I said, "Do you have any idea what it might feel like to be a foster child?" They said, "Gee, you don't have your family. You don't have your same neighborhood." They started feeling compassion.

Then I said, "How many of you would be willing to help Stephen?" Every hand went up. I said, "Okay, what kinds of things could you do to help Stephen?" They came up with a long list of things on the board: play with him at recess, walk to and from school with him, have lunch with him, and help him with his work. Then I said, "Okay, who would be willing to do each one of these?" I got specific names after each one of their suggestions.

Later I talked to Stephen. "Stephen, we talked about some of the problems you've been having in class. How many kids do you think wanted to help you?" He said, "Probably none of 'em." I said, "Every one." And he said incredulously, "Every one?" He couldn't believe it.

I want to ask you a question. Do you think Stephen's behavior changed when all the kids in that class had changed their way of thinking about him and decided to help? I can guarantee you his behavior changed significantly. When you help kids understand and get into the helping mode rather than hurting, it makes a huge difference. They are able to accomplish more than any one teacher, foster parent, principal, or counselor. The kids are powerful in what they can do to help.

The next story is regarding a Class Meeting I visited in San Bernardino, California, and a little boy I'll call Phillip. The class discussed four items while I was there. Three of them had to do with Phillip. I asked him, "Do you feel like the kids are helping you?" He just grinned and said, "Yeah, they're helping me." Later the teacher said to me, "Phillip is still the biggest behavior problem in our class, but the kids do try to help him instead of using him as a scapegoat."

Have you noticed that there is always at least one behavior-problem student in every classroom? Is there anybody who does not have one in his or her classroom? And have you ever noticed that if that child should happen to move, somebody will gladly take his or her place? There is usually one child who decides to be "special" that way. This teacher said, "The thing I like is that even though Phillip still presents most of the problems, the kids really are working with him in ways that are helpful. They really do try to help him instead of always ganging up on him, hurting him, and putting him down."

Q. *How do we guide the children into coming up with appropriate solutions?*

JANICE: I think just by talking it through with them. One of my favorite examples is an experience with a little boy who put things in his mouth all the time. Somebody put that on the agenda because it wasn't safe: he might choke. One student said, "Well, you should put his color on purple." At that time I had a color chart, and when they got down to purple, they would go see the principal. But another said, "Well, that's not going to do him any good because even if he goes to the principal, he's still going to put things in his mouth. He's still going to choke." They were thinking things through.

PRESENTER: Because you ask questions like "How is that going to help?"

KAY: I find virtually the same thing with the fourth graders. A lot of times I ask them, "Is this reasonable? And is it related to the problem?" And they will go back to it and say, "Oh, well, one of these is not related." And they will discuss which ones are not related and mark them off the list. So they really do a lot of thinking before they choose a solution.

I've also often found that the first time a problem appears on the agenda, the students' solution is to stop the behavior. Frequently, that's all that's needed. All they need to know is that the behavior is a problem to one of their peers. It is very important to them to have peer approval. If they know that something is displeasing to their peers, many times all they will do is say, "I'll stop it." And it does stop.

PRESENTER: So in other words, sometimes just a discussion is enough. I really want to emphasize this. So often people focus too much on consequences or solutions without realizing the power of letting the kids discuss it. After you discuss it, you can say, "Okay, if this happens again, it can go on the agenda." But you might be surprised how often it won't happen again.

Asking questions such as "How will that help?" can be very powerful in teaching kids to consider long-range results. Also, it helps to have the slogan "We're here to help each other, not to hurt each other." Sometimes you can ask these questions: "How many of you feel like we're coming up with suggestions that are helpful?" "How many of you think we're coming up with suggestions that are hurtful?" A key technique, whenever you see things going wrong, is to ask a question. But ask it both ways: "How many of you think we're being too noisy?" "How many of you think it's quiet enough?" "How many of you think we're being respectful?" "How many of you think we're being disrespectful?" Asking questions invites students to think.

Q. How do we handle children who use the agenda as revenge?

KAY: In the beginning, I did find that the children used the agenda for revenge all the time. So I came up with an agenda box. It has a hole in the top, and they put their agenda item in the box. They created a number system. They put a number on the problem, then crossed off the number they used so the next person would know which number to use, and we took them in order at the Class Meeting. So it works beautifully! The children love it, and they're in charge of taking care of it all. I don't do any of it.

PRESENTER: With this system you can keep problems that go in the box in order. That's brilliant!

JANICE: I don't notice that first graders use the agenda for revenge. I just find that they're pretty honest. Usually, a classmate will check on them and say, "She just did that to get back." When I confront them, they'll usually say, "Yeah, I did." I always like to thank them or give them credit for admitting something like that right away.

PRESENTER: Any one of these questions could go on the agenda. You could ask them, "What should we do about people using the agenda for revenge?" They will come up with great answers. But the other thing is that whenever you have a problem, talk about it openly with the kids.

Another way to handle the kids using the agenda for revenge is to say, "I've noticed that we're using the agenda for revenge." Then I would ask some questions like, "How many think that we don't trust each other yet to know that we're here to help each other rather than hurt each other?" Getting the students involved in solutions or a simple discussion is usually enough to stop the revenge.

Q. How do you incorporate other discipline strategies with the Positive Discipline program?

PRESENTER: I have a generic answer for that: it fits any other discipline program that treats kids with dignity and respect, that is not humiliating, that works for solutions rather than blame, and that teaches skills rather than punishment and control. It does not fit discipline programs that are based on a punishment-reward premise. That is a totally opposite premise. Those systems teach adults to be responsible for kids' behavior by catching kids when they're "good" and rewarding them and catching kids when they're "bad" and punishing them. But what happens when the adult is not around? It also is a short-term control, rather than taking a look at what children are feeling and deciding and what kind of skills they are learning for future behavior.

Do you want to make any closing comments? I would like to hear from both of you, just a summarization about what you think about the whole thing.

KAY: Holding regularly scheduled Class Meetings is one of the most wonderful things that's ever happened to me in my classroom, and my students feel the same way. They love it! They fuss if we miss a Class Meeting. I have Class Meetings every day. Once in a while our schedule becomes so hectic, we just can't work it in that day, and they really miss it. I find that my classroom operates much more smoothly if we have the opportunity to have the compliments. If we don't have time for anything except compliments, even that makes the day run much more smoothly.

PRESENTER: I'm so glad you mentioned that. So many teachers say that the whole day runs more smoothly when they do have Class Meetings, even if it's only the compliment part.

JANICE: I love Class Meetings. I urge everyone to try it. I never felt comfortable with the discipline program we had when I came into the system. I was so glad to be able to take something that would replace it. I have nothing in place in my classroom now for discipline except Class Meetings.

• • •

We hope this transcript has captured the expertise, positive attitude, and outstanding skills of Janice Ritter and Kay Rogers. We believe their examples will be an inspiration to thousands of teachers who see the potential of Class Meetings for empowering students and creating a cooperative classroom climate. We hope you, too, will be motivated by their experience to start Class Meetings and enjoy the fruits of this powerful process for teachers and students alike.

CONCLUSION

I have fallen into the world, and will now have to swim.

RUDOLF DREIKURS

Now that you have read the book, where will you go from here? If you have the courage to be imperfect and are willing to make mistakes, you can institute Positive Discipline in your classrooms, learning along with your students.

Tammy Keces, elementary school teacher and parent educator for over twenty years (and now a certified Positive Discipline trainer), summarizes her experiences with Positive Discipline this way:

"Through my work with teachers, parents, educators, therapists, doctors, nurses, lawyers, scientists et al., over the last three years since I learned about Positive Discipline, I have come to see that it includes the most comprehensive and useful set of life skills and tools one can have today. PD can be used to create consistently more peaceful, productive, and empowering relationships among children and adults of all ages, ethnic backgrounds, and religions.

"In the classroom, PD has transformed how I communicate with students, built supportive connections with all members of the classroom regardless of the type of learner, put the emphasis on creating a respectful, supportive classroom community, instilled reflective, self-regulatory behavior as a way of discipline, and inspired a desire for students to be intrinsically motivated to achieve academic and social success. Overall, the classroom became a nurturing, joyful, happy place to learn and grow. As a teacher, I was excited to apply the PD philosophy to creating new PD lessons connected to the general curriculum. Parents and students have thrived and shone in the Positive Discipline classroom.

"For me personally, PD has been equally as compelling in how the tools for parenting have shaped better communication, closer relationships, and mutual respect in my home. Introducing Family Meetings invited meaningful discussion, a platform for individual concerns and questions to be addressed, and a safe place simply to be heard. The Family Meeting has now been integrated into the daily life of our family. The PD tools for communication can be used in a multitude of scenarios and is grounded in respectful communication.

"Building the home and school bridge has created a rewarding dynamic with teachers, parents, and students alike. Walking through the Mistaken Goals Chart with parents has been an eye-opening, and often tearful, realization of how we as adults can move a child from his or her space of negative attention-seeking behavior to one of encouragement and understanding. Holding regular workshops with parents to teach the same tools that the children are learning in the class has become a key component to Positive Discipline making the biggest impact.

"Parents reverting back to the behavioral modification approach, extrinsically *rewarding* their children with monetary rewards, token material objects, or empty praise would turn up at my door frustrated by the short-term results. Positive Discipline offered the critical difference in making a significant change in children's behavior. A great example of this was when my own ten-year-old son Colby kindly declined a *reward* his teacher offered to him after doing a *good job* on his work and said, 'I don't need the prize because I feel really good about what I did.' His teacher was nothing short of shocked at his refusal of her *positive reinforcement*. The greatest gift you give children is when their own effort, determination, and *feeling* of pride becomes the ultimate prize!"

Our wish is that you, like Tammy, find your path with the help of Positive Discipline to positively influence your world and the world of your students. We look forward to hearing about your successes. Send us your stories of Positive Discipline in Action to jane@positivediscipline .com or lynnlott@sbcglobal.net so we can share them with others and inspire teachers to jump on the Positive Discipline train for social emotional development and academic achievement.

ACKNOWLEDGMENTS

We'd like to acknowledge our project editor, Nathan Roberson. He has been exceptionally quick to respond to our every need and guides us with such patience.

Thanks to Paula Gray for bringing our text alive with her delightful illustrations, and Adam DeVito for his illustrations of the Wheel of Choice Mobiles and the Icebergs.

We also want to thank the many teachers and administrators who provide valuable feedback on how useful our ideas are in creating the classrooms they desire. We share some of their stories in this book.

We can never show enough thanks for the Positive Discipline Association (www.positivediscipline.org) and the Certified Positive Discipline Trainers and Lead Trainers and all that they do to provide training and ongoing support for the many dedicated and passionate people who are sharing Positive Discipline with parents and teachers all over the world.

BIBLIOGRAPHY

Adler, Alfred. *Cooperation Between the Sexes*. New York: Anchor Books, 1978.

———. *Social Interest*. New York: Capricorn Books, 1964.

———. *Superiority and Social Interest*. Evanston, IL: Northwestern University Press, 1964.

———. *What Life Should Mean to You*. New York: Capricorn Books, 1958.

Albert, Linda. *Coping with Kids*. New York: E. P. Dutton, 1982.

Ansbacher, Heinz, and Rowena Ansbacher. *The Individual Psychology of Alfred Adler*. New York: Harper Torchbooks, 1964.

Beecher, Willard, and Marguerite Beecher. *Beyond Success and Failure*. New York: Pocket Books, 1966.

Bettner, Betty Lou, and Amy Lew. *Raising Kids Who Can*. New York: HarperCollins, 1992.

Charles, C. M. *Building Classroom Discipline,* 6th edition. New York: Longman, 1998.

Christianson, Oscar. *Adlerian Family Counseling*. Minneapolis, MN: Educational Media, 1983.

Corsini, Raymond, and Genevieve Painter. *The Practical Parent*. New York: Harper and Row, 1975.

Dinkmeyer, Don, and Rudolf Dreikurs. *Encouraging Children to Learn: The Encouragement Process.* Englewood Cliffs, NJ: Prentice-Hall, 1963.

Dinkmeyer, Don, and Gary McKay. *Parents Handbook: Systematic Training for Effective Parenting,* 3rd edition. Circle Pines, MN: American Guidance Service, 1989.

———. *Raising a Responsible Child.* New York: Simon & Schuster, 1978.

Dinkmeyer, Don, and W. L. Pew. *Adlerian Counseling and Psychotherapy.* Monterey, CA: Brooks/Cole, 1979.

Dreikurs, Rudolf. *Psychology in the Classroom.* New York: Harper and Row, 1966.

———. *Social Equality: The Challenge of Today.* Chicago: Contemporary Books, 1971.

Dreikurs, Rudolf, Raymond Corsini, and S. Gould. *Family Council.* Chicago: Henry Regnery, 1974.

Dreikurs, Rudolf, Bernice Grunwald, and Floyd Pepper. *Maintaining Sanity in the Classroom,* 2nd edition. Accelerated Development, 1998.

Dreikurs, Rudolf, and V. Soltz. *Children: The Challenge.* Plume, 1991.

Glenn, H. Stephen. *Developing Capable People* (audiotape/videotape sets). Orem, UT: Empowering People Books, Tapes & Videos. (1-800-456-7770)

———. *Developing Healthy Self-Esteem* (audiotape/videotape). Orem, UT: Empowering People Books, Tapes & Videos, 1989. (1-800-456-7770)

———. *Involving and Motivating People* (audiotape). Orem, UT: Empowering People Books, Tapes & Videos, 1986. (1-800-456-7770)

———. *Teachers Who Make a Difference* (audiotape/videotape). Orem, UT: Empowering People Books, Tapes & Videos, 1989. (1-800-456-7770)

Glenn, H. Stephen, and Michael L. Brock. *7 Strategies for Developing Capable Students,* Rocklin, CA: Prima, 1998.

Glenn, H. Stephen, and Jane Nelsen. *Raising Self-Reliant Children in a Self-Indulgent World.* Rocklin, CA: Prima Publishing, 1988.

Kohn, Alfie. *Punished by Rewards*. New York: Houghton Mifflin, 1993.

Kvols, Kathy. *Redirecting Children's Misbehavior.* Seattle: Parenting Press, 1997.

Lott, Lynn, and Riki Intner. *Chores Without Wars*. Rocklin, CA: Prima Publishing, 1998.

Lott, Lynn, Riki Intner, and Barbara Mendenhall, *Do-It-Yourself Therapy: How to Think, Feel, and Act Like a New Person in Just 8 Weeks*. Franklin Lakes, NJ: Career Press, 1999.

Lott, Lynn, and Jane Nelsen. *Teaching Parenting the Positive Discipline Way* (a manual). Orem, UT: Empowering People Books, Tapes & Videos, 1990. (1-800-456-7770)

Manaster, Guy J., and Raymond Corsini. *Individual Psychology*. Itasca, IL: F. E. Peacock Publishers, 1982.

Nelsen, Jane. *From Here to Serenity: Four Principles for Understanding Who You Really Are*. Roseville, CA: Prima Publishing, 2000.

———. *Positive Discipline*. New York: Ballantine Books, 1996.

———. *Positive Discipline* (audiotape). Orem, UT: Empowering People Books, Tapes & Videos, 1988. (1-800-456-7770)

———. *Positive Discipline* (videotape set). Orem, UT: Empowering People Books, Tapes & Videos, 1988. (1-800-456-7770)

———. *Positive Time-Out and 50 Other Ways to Avoid Power Struggles in Homes and Schools*. Rocklin, CA: Prima Publishing, 1999.

Nelsen, Jane, Roslyn Duffy, and Cheryl Erwin. *Positive Discipline the First Three Years*. Rocklin, CA: Prima Publishing, 1998.

———. *Positive Discipline for Preschoolers*. Rocklin, CA: Prima Publishing, 1998.

Nelsen, Jane, Roslyn Duffy, Linda Escobar, Kate Ortolano, and Debbie Owen-Sohocki. *Positive Discipline: A Teacher's A–Z Guide*. Rocklin, CA: Prima Publishing, 1996.

Nelsen, Jane, Cheryl Erwin, and Carol Delzer. *Positive Discipline for Single Parents*. Rocklin, CA: Prima Publishing, 1999.

Nelsen, Jane, Riki Intner, and Lynn Lott. *Positive Discipline for Parenting in Recovery* (previously published as *Clean and Sober Parenting*). Rocklin, CA: Prima Publishing, 1996.

Nelsen, Jane, and Lynn Lott. *Positive Discipline for Teenagers,* revised 2nd edition. Roseville, CA: Prima Publishing, 2000.

Nelsen, Jane, Lynn Lott, and H. Stephen Glenn. *Positive Discipline: A–Z.* Rocklin, CA: Prima Publishing, 1999.

———. *Positive Discipline in the Classroom.* Roseville, CA: Prima Publishing, 2000.

Pew, W. L., and J. Terner. *Courage to Be Imperfect.* New York: Hawthorn Books, 1978.

Smith, Manuel J. *When I Say No I Feel Guilty.* New York: The Dial Press, 1975.

Video Journal of Education, The. "Positive Discipline in the Classroom." Program One: "A Foundation for Positive Discipline." Program Two: "Class Meetings, the Forum of Positive Discipline." Sandy, UT: *The Video Journal of Education,* volume VI, issue 7, 1997. (1-800-572-1153)

Walton, F. X. *Winning Teenagers Over.* Columbia, SC: Adlerian Child Care Books.

INDEX

ABOUT THE AUTHORS

JANE NELSEN is the author and coauthor of twenty books and is a licensed family therapist with a doctorate in educational psychology from the University of San Francisco. She finds much of her material as the mother of seven children, twenty-two grandchildren, and two great grandchildren—and a very supportive husband. She wrote the first Positive Discipline book in 1981. Later she teamed up with Lynn Lott to write *Positive Discipline for Teenagers, Positive Discipline A–Z, Positive Discipline in the Classroom, Positive Discipline for Parenting in Recovery,* and *When Your Dog Is Like Family* (an ebook). Many books in the Positive Discipline series have followed, and now have a following of thousands in many languages.

LYNN LOTT is the author and coauthor of eighteen books and is a licensed family therapist with a master's degree in marriage and family counseling from the University of San Francisco (1978) and a master's degree in psychology from Sonoma State University (1977). She has been in private practice since 1978 helping parents, couples, teens, and individuals and now does therapy with clients all over the world through Skype. In her spare time, Lynn is an avid skier, reader, cook, and hiker. She resides in California and Florida with her husband, Hal Penny. Lynn is the mother of two, stepmother of two, and grandmother of six. For more information about Lynn, visit www.lynnlott.com.

Together, Lynn and Jane have created training workshops in Teaching Parenting the Positive Discipline Way and Positive Discipline in the Classroom. Dates and locations for these live workshops (and the DVD training formats for people unable to travel to live workshops) can be found at www.positivediscipline.com, where information also can be found about parenting classes taught by Certified Positive Discipline Parent Educators in the United States and other countries.

FROM PRESCHOOLER TO A REBELLIOUS TEENAGER, WE HAVE THE POSITIVE DISCIPLINE SOLUTIONS YOU NEED

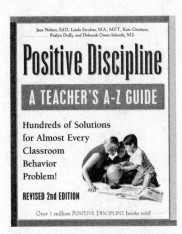
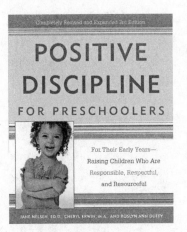

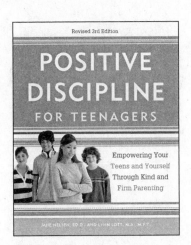